THE HUMANITARIAN CRISIS IN SYRIA: VIEWS FROM THE GROUND

HEARING

BEFORE THE

SUBCOMMITTEE ON
THE MIDDLE EAST AND NORTH AFRICA

OF THE

COMMITTEE ON FOREIGN AFFAIRS
HOUSE OF REPRESENTATIVES

ONE HUNDRED THIRTEENTH CONGRESS

SECOND SESSION

MAY 21, 2014

Serial No. 113–149

Printed for the use of the Committee on Foreign Affairs

Available via the World Wide Web: http://www.foreignaffairs.house.gov/ or
http://www.gpo.gov/fdsys/

U.S. GOVERNMENT PRINTING OFFICE

88–019PDF   WASHINGTON : 2014

For sale by the Superintendent of Documents, U.S. Government Printing Office
Internet: bookstore.gpo.gov   Phone: toll free (866) 512–1800; DC area (202) 512–1800
Fax: (202) 512–2104   Mail: Stop IDCC, Washington, DC 20402–0001

COMMITTEE ON FOREIGN AFFAIRS

EDWARD R. ROYCE, California, *Chairman*

CHRISTOPHER H. SMITH, New Jersey
ILEANA ROS-LEHTINEN, Florida
DANA ROHRABACHER, California
STEVE CHABOT, Ohio
JOE WILSON, South Carolina
MICHAEL T. McCAUL, Texas
TED POE, Texas
MATT SALMON, Arizona
TOM MARINO, Pennsylvania
JEFF DUNCAN, South Carolina
ADAM KINZINGER, Illinois
MO BROOKS, Alabama
TOM COTTON, Arkansas
PAUL COOK, California
GEORGE HOLDING, North Carolina
RANDY K. WEBER SR., Texas
SCOTT PERRY, Pennsylvania
STEVE STOCKMAN, Texas
RON DeSANTIS, Florida
DOUG COLLINS, Georgia
MARK MEADOWS, North Carolina
TED S. YOHO, Florida

ELIOT L. ENGEL, New York
ENI F.H. FALEOMAVAEGA, American
  Samoa
BRAD SHERMAN, California
GREGORY W. MEEKS, New York
ALBIO SIRES, New Jersey
GERALD E. CONNOLLY, Virginia
THEODORE E. DEUTCH, Florida
BRIAN HIGGINS, New York
KAREN BASS, California
WILLIAM KEATING, Massachusetts
DAVID CICILLINE, Rhode Island
ALAN GRAYSON, Florida
JUAN VARGAS, California
BRADLEY S. SCHNEIDER, Illinois
JOSEPH P. KENNEDY III, Massachusetts
AMI BERA, California
ALAN S. LOWENTHAL, California
GRACE MENG, New York
LOIS FRANKEL, Florida
TULSI GABBARD, Hawaii
JOAQUIN CASTRO, Texas

AMY PORTER, *Chief of Staff*   THOMAS SHEEHY, *Staff Director*
JASON STEINBAUM, *Democratic Staff Director*

————

SUBCOMMITTEE ON THE MIDDLE EAST AND NORTH AFRICA

ILEANA ROS-LEHTINEN, Florida, *Chairman*

STEVE CHABOT, Ohio
JOE WILSON, South Carolina
ADAM KINZINGER, Illinois
TOM COTTON, Arkansas
RANDY K. WEBER SR., Texas
RON DeSANTIS, Florida
DOUG COLLINS, Georgia
MARK MEADOWS, North Carolina
TED S. YOHO, Florida

THEODORE E. DEUTCH, Florida
GERALD E. CONNOLLY, Virginia
BRIAN HIGGINS, New York
DAVID CICILLINE, Rhode Island
ALAN GRAYSON, Florida
JUAN VARGAS, California
BRADLEY S. SCHNEIDER, Illinois
JOSEPH P. KENNEDY III, Massachusetts
GRACE MENG, New York
LOIS FRANKEL, Florida

CONTENTS

Page

WITNESSES

LETTERS, STATEMENTS, ETC., SUBMITTED FOR THE HEARING

APPENDIX

THE HUMANITARIAN CRISIS IN SYRIA: VIEWS FROM THE GROUND

WEDNESDAY, MAY 21, 2014

House of Representatives,
Subcommittee on the Middle East and North Africa,
Committee on Foreign Affairs,
Washington, DC.

The subcommittee met, pursuant to notice, at 2 o'clock p.m., in room 2172, Rayburn House Office Building, Hon. Ileana Ros-Lehtinen (chairman of the subcommittee) presiding.

Ms. Ros-Lehtinen. Thank you so much. The subcommittee will come to order. Unfortunately—well, fortunately, we will be interrupted by votes because I like to be interrupted by democracy. That is always a good thing. But after recognizing myself and ranking member, my good friend Ted Deutch from Florida, for 5 minutes each for our opening statements, I will then recognize other members seeking recognition for 1 minute each. We will then hear from our witnesses.

Thank you, ladies and gentlemen, for joining us. Without objection, the prepared statements of all of our witnesses will be made a part of the record and members may have 5 days in which to insert statements and questions for the record subject to the length limitation in the rules. The chair now recognizes herself for 5 minutes.

It is a tragedy that, unfortunately, we are all too familiar with. By now we have seen the images and heard the unimaginable stories of despair, of horror, of suffering, and we know all too well the alarming numbers. More than 150,000 people have been killed as a result of Assad's war to stay in power. Nearly 3 million people have fled from Syria into neighboring countries, such as Jordan, Lebanon, Turkey, Iraq, creating instability within those countries as they struggle to cope with the strains that this massive influx of refugees has placed on their security and their stability; 6.5 million, that is the number of internally displaced persons, IDPs in Syria, and 10 million, that is roughly the number of people in dire need of humanitarian assistance, and sadly, the vast majority of those hit hardest by this crisis are the women and children of Syria.

We are here today to get an important assessment from those who are on the ground who try to meet the needs of the millions of Syrians in desperate need of assistance. I would like to say thank you on behalf of our subcommittee to each and every one of you for the valuable work that you do. People who need your help and have the courage to come here today, thank you, and I know that comes at great risk.

So far, the administration's approach to resolving the Syrian conflict leaves much to be desired by any metric. Unless the administration addresses the underlying root causes for this humanitarian disaster, we are likely to be here again next year and in the years to come asking the very same heart-wrenching questions. Getting chemical weapons out of Syria is a vital step forward, but more importantly, we must be working together to ensure that Assad leaves power so that his reign of terror ends. These past 3 years plus, the administration has been plagued by inaction, by indecisiveness, by the inability or perhaps unwillingness to put into motion a policy plan that will lead to an end to this unthinkable human tragedy, and the time for half measures and fence sitting has long ago passed.

We have been reactionary far too often where we should have been proactive. Our response has been to provide humanitarian assistance, and we will continue to provide it as long as millions continue to suffer needlessly, but that is never going to solve the problem. It is like trying to plug the holes in a sinking ship; short-term solutions to a much larger long-term problem. Syria is becoming the training grounds for violent extremists, destabilizing the entire region, endangering the security of our ally, the democratic Jewish State of Israel, and posing a threat to our own national security interests in the region as well.

To date the United States has allocated over $1.7 billion to meet the humanitarian needs stemming from the Syrian crisis, nearly a quarter of all international contributions to Syria, and in his budget request for Fiscal Year 2015, the President has requested an additional $1.1 billion.

We have with us today representatives of the five nongovernmental organizations who have helped serve as important, vital implementing partners, both in Syria and in the neighboring countries. The work that these NGOs do is important, vitally important, but it is also extremely dangerous, and as the ones who have to face the obstacles on the ground, it is vital that we hear directly from them about how effective our U.S. assistance has been with the hope of reaching as many people as possible.

Just last week, the Associated Press ran a disturbing article on how corruption is seeping into the aid process for Syrian refugees. It tells the story of Syrian women who are forced to bribe middlemen in order to access some of the aid because some of the areas are just too difficult to enter for some of the NGOs or they simply just don't have the manpower to do it. So they rely on these middlemen to be honest brokers, and it seems that they are exploiting the loopholes in the system. And it is stories like these that show us how important today's hearing is so that we can better understand exactly what is happening on the ground.

I look forward to hearing from our witnesses, these implementing partners, and what they have to go through in order to disperse the humanitarian aid that we provide and learn from them what more we can do so that we can better ensure that more people are getting the assistance that they so desperately need.

And with that I am pleased to yield to my ranking member, my friend, Mr. Deutch of Florida.

Mr. DEUTCH. Thank you, Madam Chairman.

I would like to take a moment to offer my sincere thanks to the witnesses for being here today. Your organizations are quite literally on the front lines, and while we continue to debate policy actions here in Washington, it is the aid workers that risk their lives every single day to provide some relief to those suffering under the most horrendous human conditions. We owe each and every one of them our deepest gratitude, and we thank you for being here today.

Syria is an extraordinary challenge in terms of sheer numbers of those in need, the lack of resources, and access, and the devastating levels of violence. In less than 2 months, the death toll has risen by 10,000, meaning over 160,000 people have lost their lives in this conflict. The number has risen so dramatically and access to so many parts of the country is limited, the United Nations can no longer keep an official death count. Inside Syria 6.5 million people have been displaced; nearly 10 million are in need of aid. The U.N. recently estimated that close to 250,000 of these people were unreachable because their communities were caught directly in the middle of the fighting, and there are now 2.8 million refugees. I know we have heard these figures before, but they bear repeating because the world needs to be reminded over and over again of the enormity of this conflict. There are nearly 1,070,000 refugees in Lebanon, 740,000 in Turkey, 600,000 in Jordan, 225,000 in Iraq, and 137,000 in Egypt.

The United States, as the largest donor of aid to the United Nations, has a responsibility to help ensure humanitarian access. U.N. Security Council Resolution 2139, which demanded that all parties, in particular the Syrian authorities, promptly allow rapid, safe, and unhindered humanitarian access for agencies and their implementing partners, including across conflict lines and across borders, is not being implemented. All of the parties to the conflict, including the Assad regime and the network of nonstate actors, must abide by this resolution and allow for humanitarian aid to reach the Syrian people unobstructed.

The situation inside Syria is dire. Food deliveries are held due to eruptions of violence, reports of middlemen exchanging bribes for aid and simply not enough medical professionals to provide care. Children are going without needed vaccinations, sparking new cases of polio and measles, diseases that had all but been eradicated in Syria. An entire generation of Syrian children may not attend school because their school no longer exists in Syria or they need to work to support their now refugee families.

In Lebanon, where Syria refugees make up one-quarter of the population, the school system can't physically support the influx of over 400,000 children. Furthermore, Syrian children are stymied by language barriers as they are not often used to learning in English or in French. I know that several of the organizations here today are specifically focused on children's needs, and I look forward to hearing more about your efforts to prevent a lost generation.

In Jordan, the Zaatari refugee camp is now housing upwards of 120,000 refugees on any given day. Inside the camp we have seen reports of sexual assault, trafficking, and child marriages, and young men exposed to radicalization or enticed by opposition groups to return to fight in the conflict.

We have spent the better part of 3 years now debating United States' response and policy prescriptions for Syria. For 3 years, we have been told these are really hard decisions that we have to make. There may not be good decisions. It is just really difficult for us to decide. The choices are hard, but we have to make them. We need to make hard choices, and we need to make them now.

I am pleased that the London 11 Group last week recognized that changes in access and speed of our humanitarian aid need to be made and made fast. I hope that this includes the U.N. Security Council addressing the issue of cross-border aid. We must get the international community to pay attention to what is happening inside Syria. I am frustrated at the pace of humanitarian response, and quite frankly the lack of funding is appalling. The U.N. has requested $6.5 billion for humanitarian aid this year, yet only $1.2 billion has been pledged by the international community. In total, since the conflict has begun, the U.S. has given $1.7 billion. The world simply cannot turn a blind eye to over 9 million people in need. This crisis will not end, will not end even if a political situation is somehow reached; 2.8 million will fundamentally alter the landscape of the region for decades. Entire communities in Syria will need to be rebuilt before refugees can even think of returning home.

I hope that this hearing today will continue to shine a light on the enormity and the significance of what is happening in and around Syria. Again, I want to extend my sincere thanks and my profound gratitude to each of your organizations and the thousands of aid workers who put their lives at risk each and every day to provide relief to those suffering the most unimaginable horrors of war.

Thank you, Madam Chairman. I yield back.

Ms. ROS-LEHTINEN. Thank you very much for a very eloquent statement. Thank you, Mr. Deutch.

I am pleased to yield to another one of our subcommittee chairmen, Mr. Chabot of Ohio.

Mr. CHABOT. Thank you, Madam Chairman, and thank you for calling this important hearing to examine one of the most significant foreign policy failures of the Obama administration.

The violence in Syria over the last few years has spiraled out of control, yielding a serious humanitarian crisis. It was in August 2012 that the President declared a red line, and today over 160,000 people have been senselessly killed. There is no end in sight to this crisis. The effort to rid Syria of chemical weapons is bogged down, and the White House has seemed to abdicate leadership on the issue. However, we know there are many Americans who care deeply about this humanitarian crisis in Syria. In fact, the organizations represented here today are working tirelessly to help the Syrian people, but they are facing serious obstacles that this administration needs to do more to ensure the better flow of goods into Syria. The U.S. needs to work closer with our friends and allies in the region, Turkey and Jordan, for example, to facilitate the movement of that cargo.

I also call on the administration to better outline what is permitted under Syrian sanctions in terms of donations and medical services. As the U.S. is the largest contributor of humanitarian assistance, we here in Congress also need to be judicious in determining who is receiving this aid in Syria and ensuring that it reaches those people who need it most and that it is not going into the hands of the Assad regime or into those that are on the opposite side of freedom.

So thank you for your leadership on this, Madam Chair, and I yield back.

Ms. ROS-LEHTINEN. Thank you so much, Mr. Chabot.

And now we are so pleased to welcome our wonderful panelists, and we are just thrilled to have you.

First we welcome Ms. Andrea Koppel—thank you—who is vice president of global engagement and policy at Mercy Corps, where she leads global advocacy on issues, including the Syrian crisis and U.S. assistance reform. She has over 25 years of communications, journalism, and advocacy experience. And she previously served as director of international communications at the American Red Cross following the 2010 Haiti earthquake.

We welcome you, Ms. Koppel.

We also have with us Ms. Holly Solberg, who is director of emergency and humanitarian assistance at CARE. Ms. Solberg has 20 years of experience in international relief and development and specifically in emergency management and humanitarian efforts. She has worked with CARE for nearly 19 years and has been based in Atlanta, Ethiopia, Mozambique, Thailand, Kenya, and Switzerland.

We welcome you, thank you.

Then we welcome Ms. Pia Wanek, who directs the Office of Humanitarian Assistance at Global Communities. She has more than 12 years of experience in the humanitarian field, having worked for USAID's Office of U.S. Foreign Disaster Assistance at State Department's Bureau of Population and at World Vision.

We welcome you. Thank you.

Fourth, we welcome Dr. Zaher Sahloul, who is president of the Syrian American Medical Society. Dr. Sahloul is a practicing critical care specialist in Chicago, and he just returned from his latest medical mission to the City of Aleppo. He has been on several medical missions to Syria, Jordan, Turkey, Lebanon, and Iraq and has also helped train medical relief workers in topics like medical practices in war zones.

Thank you, sir.

Last but not least, we welcome Ms. Bernice Romero, who is senior director for policy and advocacy at Save the Children. Before this, she was advocacy and campaigns director for OXFAM International and oversaw OXFAM's international advocacy offices in Washington, Geneva, Brussels, and New York.

This is an impressive panel. Thank you all for being here.

As you know, your written statements have been made a part of the record, so please feel free to summarize in 5 minutes. Thank you. We will begin with you.

STATEMENT OF MS. ANDREA KOPPEL, VICE PRESIDENT OF GLOBAL ENGAGEMENT AND POLICY, MERCY CORPS

Ms. KOPPEL. Thank you, Chairwoman Ros-Lehtinen, Ranking Member Deutch, Mr. Chabot, and members of the subcommittee. Thank you so much for the invitation today and for the close attention you have paid to this incredibly complex and protracted crisis now in its fourth year.

Mercy Corps is assisting the best we can in these extraordinarily difficult circumstances. For nearly 2 years, we have been delivering humanitarian assistance to civilians inside Syria through the most direct routes, reaching more than 1.7 million people who are suffering. We are among the largest providers of food and baking flour. We are leading these programs with the generous support of donors, including USAID's Emergency Food Security Program, funded through the International Disaster Assistance Account.

Every day, hundreds of my colleagues risk their lives delivering flour to Syrian bakeries to ensure that hundreds of thousands of Syrian civilians have bread to eat every day. In addition, we are also delivering a monthly supply of food staples, things like oil, beans, rice, pasta, enough to provide a family of seven with at least half their daily caloric requirements. And it is worth noting that by purchasing this food in the region, we are able to give American taxpayers more impact for their money, ensuring supplies are delivered quickly and at a lower cost, while also stimulating lower markets.

For Mercy Corps and other dedicated aid agencies, Syria poses one of the most complex, hostile, and difficult response environments in which we have ever worked, but of course these humanitarian challenges, as you have already laid out, are not confined to Syria. Massive refugee flows into neighboring countries have turned a civil conflict into a regional crisis. The pressure on host countries is immense. By the end of the year, the number of refugees is estimated, and this is just registered, to move from 2.8 to at least 4 million. Caught in the middle are children, Syrian children, Lebanese children, and Jordanian children.

With our partners UNICEF, Save the Children, World Vision, we are working to elevate the needs of children, especially adolescents to prevent, as you said, Ranking Member Deutch, what may become a lost generation. During focus group discussions that Mercy Corps had earlier this year with adolescents, we found a sense of humiliation was pervasive and often involved physical violence. Flash points with this violence revolved around disputes over wages, verbal assaults while they are playing in the neighborhood or just walking to school. One boy told us he would love to move to a country where humans are valued. ''If I cannot go there,'' he said, ''I want to leave this world.'' Another boy said, ''It would be better to return to Syria and fight and die with dignity than to continue to live here in humiliation.''

While the situation is certainly bleak, there are a number of concrete steps that Congress can take right now to help the people of Syria and neighboring countries. First, there was a desperate need for funding humanitarian assistance that also supports more strategic longer-term needs. Congress can ensure that Fiscal Year 2015 humanitarian assistance and needs are met by fully restoring IDA,

MRA, Food for Peace to Fiscal Year 2014 enacted levels and by ensuring that IDA and MRA accounts are more adaptable in order, where appropriate, to graduate emergency funds into more strategic longer-term programs that integrate both relief and development aids.

Second, Congress must urge the administration to push for, as you said, Congressman Deutch, the full implementation of U.N. Security Council Resolution 2139 and to work with the U.N. to maximize coordination and do a better job of including civil society actors in decisionmaking.

Third, humanitarian aid must not be used as a proxy for the lack of a political solution.

And, fourth, Congress should call on the administration to prioritize programs that build the resilience of refugees and host communities with a special focus on adolescents and integrated conflict mitigation.

In conclusion, I would like to say that through our work in partnerships in the region, we have been humbled and touched by the grace and the dignity of the Syrian people as well as by the generosity of their regional hosts. I wish to sincerely thank the members of this subcommittee for its focus on this tremendously important issue and for extending me the privilege of testifying here today. I would be more than willing to accept your questions later.

Ms. ROS-LEHTINEN. Thank you so much, Ms. Koppel. Thank you for your testimony.

[The prepared statement of Ms. Koppel follows:]

Statement of Andrea Koppel
Vice President, Global Engagement and Policy, Mercy Corps

U.S. House Committee on Foreign Affairs
Subcommittee on the Middle East and North Africa

Hearing on:
The Humanitarian Crisis in Syria: Views from the Ground
May 21, 2014

Chairwoman Ros-Lehtinen, Ranking Member Deutch:

Thank you for inviting me to testify before the Sub-Committee today about the growing humanitarian crisis in Syria and for the close attention you have paid to this complex and protracted crisis, which has now entered its 4th year. I am here today in my capacity as Vice President of Global Engagement and Policy with Mercy Corps, a global humanitarian and development non-governmental organization (NGO) that responds to disasters and supports community led development in more than forty countries around the world. Mercy Corps has been working in the Middle East and North Africa for over three decades; and we currently run and manage programs in nine countries in the region, inside Syria as well as in Lebanon, Jordan and Iraq.

According to the United Nations (UN), 9.3 million people are in need of assistance inside Syria, including 6.5 million internally displaced. Over half are children. Moreover, 242,000 people are estimated to be living in besieged areas where they are completely cut off from assistance or receive only limited aid. And there is no end in sight to the growing humanitarian need.

Mercy Corps is assisting the best we can in these extraordinarily difficult circumstances, and remarkably through our local partnerships we are doing so on a large scale. For nearly two years, Mercy Corps has been delivering humanitarian aid to civilians in Syria through the most direct routes, reaching more than 1.7 million civilians who are suffering.

We are among the largest providers of food and baking flour. We are leading these programs with the generous support of donors, including the important contributions of the United States Agency for International Development's Emergency Food Security Program, funded through the International Disaster Assistance (IDA) account which is administered by Food for Peace.

Every day hundreds of my colleagues risk their lives delivering flour to Syrian bakeries to ensure that hundreds of thousands of civilians will have bread to eat. In addition, we are also delivering a monthly supply of food staples: rice, bulgur wheat, pasta, lentils, canned tuna fish and other items -- enough to provide a family of seven with half their daily caloric requirements. And it's worth noting that by purchasing this food in the region, we are able to give American taxpayers more impact for their money ensuring supplies are delivered quickly and at a lower cost while also stimulating local markets.

We're also running a pilot program to buy food and non-food items inside Syria. This initiative is currently a comparatively small element of our overall procurement but is laying the groundwork for future operations. And with funding from USAID's Office of Foreign Disaster Assistance (OFDA), we are also providing civilians with essential items such as blankets, clothing, winter survival kits, hygiene items, emergency water and sanitation. Recently, we've also begun to pilot a new voucher program with pre-cleared vendors; this should give people living in areas that are frequently inaccessible due to fighting the ability to purchase what they need in their own neighborhoods.

I had the opportunity to visit Syria last year, and met with some of the families who are benefitting from this assistance. These are families who had lost everything – their homes, jobs, and belongings, but more importantly, they have also lost loved ones, friends and neighbors.

As we drove across the countryside, in what used to be the bread basket of Syria, I could not help but notice rows of tree stumps lining fields where there used to be lush olive groves. Olive groves are not only an important source of income for Syrians. They are a symbol of identity and home: an olive grove is cared for by generation after generation. These trees are, for many, a source of proud family history, a link from grandparents to grandchildren. And yet during my visit, I could see Syrians chopping down these trees. Without fuel for heat, they were burning their trees to stay warm. Or they sold the wood for cash. It was a short-term solution to a long-term crisis; a painful, and very personal accommodation to a harsh reality.

During my visit I met with a mother of four. She had fled Aleppo city along with her husband and children. This was their third temporary home. When we met, they were camping out in a tiny cinderblock garage. We sat together on the cold concrete floor where she apologized for not serving me tea. She explained they were just barely getting by. Two years into the war, they had already exhausted their life savings. The monthly food basket they received to supplement their diet -- thanks to the Food for Peace program -- was greatly appreciated, but it was not enough. They were always hungry. And so each day, this mother would send her children to go scavenging for food. Wild grasses and plants were usually the only edible things they could find. They also made small beaded decorations for shoes to sell in the market.

Despite their bleak circumstances, she said, they were among the best off in this community. She pointed toward the local school down the road, where dozens of less fortunate families, many with sick children, had crammed into abandoned classrooms. They all shared a single communal bathroom, burning wood from the desks to keep warm.

It has been over 444 days since I made that trip to Syria. And the situation has only gotten worse. Much worse.

Humanitarian aid is limited, but Mercy Corps, working with our local partners, continues to deliver vital assistance despite the dangers and challenges. There are many stories of heroism. To ensure the delivery of lifesaving assistance to desperate families caught in the siege, average Syrians – who were until just two or three years ago: economics professors, journalists, teachers, and merchants – now risk their lives every day. Delivering food in the midst of a war is incredibly dangerous work. It requires men and women who can move back and forth across the front lines, through areas of extreme violence. Mercy Corps is extremely proud to partner with many of these people. They inspire us. And they thank us. The Syrian people, they say, greatly appreciate the assistance of the United States and other donors, and yet they say much more needs to be done.

For Mercy Corps and other dedicated aid agencies, Syria poses one of the most hostile, complex and difficult response environments in which we have ever worked.

Regional Humanitarian Context

But of course these humanitarian challenges are not confined to Syria. Massive refugee flows into neighboring countries have turned a civil conflict into a regional crisis.

Now as we enter into the fourth year of the crisis, the social, political and economic landscape of Syria's neighbors is being dramatically altered by the continued influx of refugees. Currently, there are 2.8 million registered refugees. But the number is rapidly expanding and doesn't include hundreds of thousands of unregistered men, women and children. By the end of the year, the UN estimates that the total number of registered refugees will reach four million.

The pressure on host countries is immense. Those struggling the most are Lebanon and Jordan. One in four people living in Lebanon today is Syrian. In Jordan, it is one in ten. Scarce natural and financial resources are being stretched thin. Competition for jobs, rising food and rent prices and overcrowded schools and hospitals are stoking tensions between host communities and refugees. But it's also put host governments and their citizens at loggerheads.
Our recent research on water scarcity in Jordan found that the huge influx of refugees into the Kingdom of Jordan is draining natural resources and is undercutting the long-term sustainability of Jordan's water supply networks.[1]

Caught in the middle in all the affected countries are the children – host and refugee alike.

With our partners - UNICEF, Save the Children and World Vision - we are working to elevate the needs of children, helping them work through stress and trauma to find meaningful outlets for their skills and energy. We are working to prevent what may become a "lost generation."

Mercy Corps is particularly seeking strategies to ensure that adolescents - boys and girls emerging from childhood and on the threshold of adulthood – are not falling between the cracks. In all of our programming, we aim to build the capacity of local communities to address emerging needs, alleviate the impact of the crisis on natural and social resources like education and water, and defuse tensions between refugees and host communities and these communities and their national governments.

For example, our recent research on adolescents finds many are losing hope as a result of being out of school for years and unable to work legally.[2] They risk isolation from their families and

---

[1] "Tapped Out: Water Scarcity and Refugee Pressures in Jordan," online at: http://www.mercycorps.org/research-resources/tapped-out-water-scarcity-and-refugee-pressures-jordan.
[2] This report is online at: http://www.mercycorps.org/research-resources/advancing-adolescence

host communities and lack tools to deal with conflict constructively. And this is not only impacting refugees, but it's also affecting Lebanese and Jordanian youth.

For Syrian adolescents, we found a sense of humiliation was pervasive and often involved physical violence. Flashpoints for this violence revolved around disputes over wages, verbal assaults while they are playing in the neighborhood or while walking to school.

One boy told us that he would like to move to a country where humans are valued. "If I cannot go there," he said, "I want to leave this world."

Another boy said, "It would be better to return to Syria to fight and die with dignity then live with humiliation."

For adolescent girls, most especially Syrian girls, tremendous physical and social isolation is most common. One Syrian girl described her collective shelter as a "prison" where she lives under the "stifling control" of her parents, who understandably only wanted to keep her safe at home.

To help these adolescents as well as meet other long-term needs, it is imperative that the donor community shift gears and develop an integrated strategy that moves beyond the basic provision of humanitarian assistance.

Recommendations for Congress

While the situation is bleak, there are a number of concrete steps that Congress can take now to help the people of Syria, and to reduce the stress, rising tensions and destabilizing effects the crisis is putting on Syria's neighbors. I would like to leave the Sub-Committee with the following four key recommendations:

First, there is a desperate need for funding humanitarian assistance that also supports longer term needs. The vast requirements inside Syria, in addition to unexpected global challenges in countries ranging from the Central African Republic to South Sudan, have resulted in unprecedented global needs. Humanitarian funding is an important cornerstone of the US government's efforts to support stability and provide lifesaving assistance around the world and is considered, by many, to be a moral imperative. Drawing on these principles, I urge Congress to fully fund the response efforts. As of this month, the joint UN and NGO funding appeals - the Regional Response Plan (RRP) and the Syria Humanitarian Assistance Response Plan (SHARP) - are only 25 percent funded. While the US continues to lead the international community, with $1.7 billion donated to the Syria response since the start of the conflict, I was extremely disappointed and surprised to see that the Administration's FY15 budget request cut humanitarian assistance accounts by 25 percent. Congress can ensure humanitarian needs are met by restoring funding to at least $2.1 billion for International Disaster Assistance (IDA), $3.1 billion for Migration and Refugee Assistance (MRA) and $1.866 billion for Food for Peace (FFP), to address the growing needs in and around Syria. Of particular importance is the Emergency Food Security Program (EFSP), a subset of the IDA account, which has served as a stopgap against hunger for 680,000 people in Syria. Moreover, as you consider funding levels, I urge you to work with the Administration to recalibrate the response strategy to fund and integrate relief and development programming. Specifically, Congress can:

- **Encourage investments in longer-term programs – particularly for humanitarian accounts like MRA and IDA – that integrate relief and development aims.** Short-term programs alone cannot adequately address the needs of the Syrian crisis. And yet, relief programs that last only 3 to 12 months have made up the majority of the response. This is not an efficient use of funding. Short-term programs do not allow for comprehensive responses to complex needs. Lurching from one short-term plan to the next significantly undermines efficiency. It also complicates the hiring of qualified staff who are understandably reluctant to sign contracts for 3-6 month periods. In addition, it makes it difficult to establish credibility with local officials who are hesitant to build humanitarian assistance goals into their long-term planning processes when a long-term partnership is not guaranteed.

- **Shift to more integrated approach away from a "siloed" funding response – in which short-term humanitarian responses and three- to five-year development programs are kept separate.** Instead, we must implement a holistic strategy that: bridges relief and development needs; works to deliver best "value for money" outcomes; shores up the ability of front-line communities to withstand and respond to the challenges of a protracted crisis; and enables donors and implementers like Mercy Corps to efficiently marshal limited resources in response to growing, long-term needs, particularly in refugee hosting countries. This holistic strategy should also be closely aligned with national plans put forward by refugee hosting countries – including Jordan's National Resilience Plan, and Lebanon's Stabilization and Recovery Program.

- **Enhance humanitarian efforts by supporting funding for adaptable accounts, such as the Complex Crisis Fund (CCF) and the Economic Support Fund (ESF), that are nimble enough to respond to emerging issues.** Additionally, I want to call on Congress to support the Economic Support Fund (ESF) at a level of $5.1 billion and the Complex Crisis fund at a level of no less than $40 million globally. These accounts provide essential longer-term development funding to countries including Lebanon, Jordan and Iraq and protect fragile development gains previously made in these countries. While the ESF funding request for Jordan was static from FY14 to FY15, Lebanon, a country that is teetering on the brink, saw a dramatic 18 percent decrease in the President's FY15 request. Another concerning trend in US assistance is the move away from supporting Iraq. Recent events and the influx of refugees into the Kurdish Regional Government (KRG) administered areas of Iraq, layered on top of internal violence, threaten to plunge that country into a new civil war. And yet, Iraq was among the biggest losers in the FY14 budget allocation in which it's expected to receive only $23 million in US development aid—a 69 percent reduction from FY13. By FY15, the USAID Mission in Iraq plans to end all programs in the country.

Second, Congress must urge the Administration to elevate the need for the full implementation of United Nations Security Council resolution 2139. Adopted unanimously in February 2014, it demands safe and unhindered humanitarian access, across conflict lines and across borders, to people in need throughout Syria. The resolution represented an important step toward getting aid to millions of Syrians. However, it will only be meaningful if it results in real, substantial changes in Syria and if implementation is based on the practicalities and diversities of access challenges on the ground. This week we mark 90 days since 2139 was adopted and, unfortunately, we are still not seeing any tangible progress. Congress should call on Secretary of State John Kerry to fully engage with the UN to sort through legal hurdles. In addition, Congress should specifically:

- **Elevate the importance of access with the international community not only to deliver aid, but also to assess needs and monitor delivery even in conflict-affected environments.** The ability of humanitarian agencies to assess and monitor is a critical component of aid delivery and central to a 'do no harm' approach. To support this, the international community must press to allow access not only for delivery of aid, but also to assess needs and monitor impact. Moreover, we must elevate access as a tool to understanding the full breadth of needs and the impact of aid in all areas of Syria, including those that are under opposition control. While some progress has been made in the past 30 days – in that we have recently secured access to do assessments for 25 percent of the country – there are still many areas where we simply do not know the extent of the needs.

- **Encourage the Obama Administration to work with the United Nations to maximize coordination.** As the UN looks to determine its role with regards to cross border operations under the auspices of 2139's mandate, the focus of such work should be on complementing, not duplicating, the already significant efforts of NGOs working in non-Government controlled territory. Efficient delivery mechanisms and practices have been developed over the past two years – that could serve as a basis for expansion and close coordination.

- **Call for greater involvement of civil society actors in decision-making processes.** The Obama Administration must push the United Nations to include international and national non-governmental organizations in decision-making processes related to the planning of aid convoys, discussions on aid delivery mechanisms, and in the formal monitoring structures of 2139. Non-governmental actors lead a large portion of aid delivery inside Syria and have considerable expertise on the nuances of operating in the region. Discussions around 2139 – including through the High Relief Committee - risk sidelining a critical component of the aid response without the involvement of non-governmental actors.

- **Urge the Administration to ensure a quick replacement for the UN Special Envoy to Syria, Lakhdar Brahimi, who resigned this month.** This position is essential to restarting political track negotiations.

Third, humanitarian aid must not be used as a proxy for the lack of a political solution. I want to urge Congress to avoid blurring this line by using humanitarian assistance as a tool to build the legitimacy of political actors to the crisis. While it is imperative to elevate and prioritize realistic political tracks aimed at ending the conflict and moving toward a political transition, humanitarian assistance cannot play this role. For it to remain impartial and independent, humanitarian aid must remain separate from politically oriented funding. This is not just a matter of principle, but it's also a matter of security and practicality. For international NGOs like Mercy Corps, and our peers, maintaining humanitarian impartiality is central to our community-based acceptance security model. If we were to appear to take sides, our credibility, our ability to reach the people in greatest need, as well as the safety of our staff would all be at risk. Please help protect our status as humanitarian actors.

Finally, Congress should call on the Obama Administration to prioritize programs that build the resilience of refugees and host communities, with special focus on adolescents and conflict mitigation. More than 1.5 million adolescents have been affected by the conflict: boys and girls on the cusp of adulthood who are facing uncertain futures because of the shocks and stresses of war, educational disadvantages, exposure to violence, and discrimination. I want to urge Congress to increase funding for programs targeting adolescent refugees and their peers in host communities --through accounts such as MRA, IDA, ESF and CCF -- to meet their unique psychosocial and developmental needs, through programs that promote tolerance and build life skills. Through quick-impact community projects, these programs also expand economic opportunity, improve conflict management, and strengthen young people's civic engagement. Specifically, we ask Congress to call for programs that:

- **Empower local actors in fragile and transitional environments to use conflict mitigation programming to address and snuff out flash points as soon as they arise.** If addressed appropriately, crises can also foster opportunities to transform attitudes. In Mafraq, Jordan for example, during a water shortage, violence broke out between Jordanians and Syrian refugees. However, community leaders -- who were trained in conflict mitigation as part of a community infrastructure program -- negotiated with the frustrated parties, and urged the communities to remain calm until they could find a solution. After several meetings the community leaders agreed to: form a community advisory group on water; identify strategies to better maintain existing infrastructure; and coordinate their efforts with those of INGOs, local community-based organizations, and wealthy citizens to provide water tankers to the village. As a result, a downward spiral of violence was avoided and the community leaders demonstrated their ability to independently discuss and develop strategies to address contentious issues. With the protracted nature of this crisis, and the rising pressure placed on host communities, these kinds of approaches are invaluable.

- **Encourage programs funded through ESF and CCF that invest in local actors who can manage, design and implement programs that work in tandem with national response plans.** This will ensure that US interventions are not just reactive, but have a sustainable impact in the region. It will also help support our key regional allies to maintain stability and mitigate the potential for spillover of violence. This requires programs that do more than dig another well or build a new school. Programs must support existing local institutions and integrate cross-community partnerships. They should also focus on supporting the local economy and create jobs.

- **Move beyond big turn-key infrastructure projects alone and prioritize resilience oriented programming to address the roots causes of reoccurring issues that spark**

conflict. In Jordan, for example, which is a resource scarce environment, this can mean a focus on programs that help communities better deliver services like water. It also means working with the Jordanian government to streamline their own procurement procedures to cut bureaucratic tape and establish equitable investments that expand essential services – like water – to communities most in need. It also means working closely with local communities to ensure that limited water resources are conserved, and that conflicts over shortages are defused. A big part of a resilience approach must including building the capacity of local government actors and encouraging proactive consultations between the central government and those on the front lines, among them municipal governments, local committees, community-based organizations and tribal leaders.

In conclusion, I would like to say that through our work and partnerships in the region, we have been humbled and touched by the grace and dignity of Syrians as well as by the generosity of their regional hosts, despite the many profound challenges they face. We are also heartened by the unwavering faith of Syrians everywhere that there will be a peaceful resolution. It is with that goal in mind that we continue our work in the hope that soon this dreadful crisis will be over.

I wish to sincerely thank the Sub-Committee for its focus on this tremendously important issue, and for extending me the privilege of testifying today.

Ms. Ros-Lehtinen. And before we continue with our panelists, we are thrilled to announce that Mr. Royce, the chairman of the full committee, is so interested and immersed in this topic that he is joining us today, and I would like to call upon him to make statements if we may. Thank you.

Thank you, Mr. Chairman.

Mr. Royce. I thank our chairman emeritus, Ileana Ros-Lehtinen for that, and I also thank the ranking member.

We are in the fourth year of this crisis, unfortunately, and I do want to thank Eliot Engel and this committee 3 years ago for trying to get us focused and trying to push the administration and all of us to take more concerted action, and I guess the frustration that we have is that the United States and the international community continue to struggle with an issue that shouldn't have been such a struggle, which is the delivery of aid to Syrians most in need, and the problem started with delivery of aid through the regime rather than to the areas most in need. And we have solved some of that problem, but unfortunately, men, women, children have been besieged by the Assad regime now for about a year in many of these cities, and others remain isolated due to the heavy fighting between the regime and opposition groups, and a third faction now, a faction that wasn't in this when we started, and that was the terrorist organizations, the jihadists who came in from outside of the country, and this was why it was important early on to have heeded the advice of Eliot Engel and others, for the administration to have heeded the advice and gotten weaponry to the Free Syrian Army.

Now we are doing that, but we are not doing it to the extent necessary, and we have not been doing it to the extent necessary, and now we have something that Assad's regime has the audacity to implement, this kneel or starve campaign.

So the problem is not new. The U.N.'s delivery of aid solely through areas controlled by the Assad regime has been the primary obstacle early on to ensuring the delivery of aid where needed most. The U.N.'s obligations in this regard have recently been debated legally by legal experts, but it is clear that the U.N. could have much more flexibility if Russia would allow it.

So it is time to think of new solutions. The House Foreign Affairs Committee last month passed unanimously House Resolution 520, which states that the United Nations needs to find new ways of delivering that aid, including through private partners, to the Syrian people, who are being besieged. And finally, I am encouraged that Secretary Kerry is now calling for the same, and the United States has provided now $1.7 billion in humanitarian aid in response to this crisis over the last 3, and I guess it is about 3½ years through the U.N. Our concern for the Syrian people and our stewardship of these taxpayer dollars requires that we ensure the intended delivery of the assistance it funds. We need to be much more emphatic about that.

Alarmingly, the Assad regime has not stopped at blocking aid, but its forces routinely target humanitarian workers and facilities, especially those providing medical care to suffering Syrians. They target them with snipers. They have killed doctors. They target them with shelling, and of course, as you are reading, with barrel bombs, and somebody needs to say something more about the additional chemical attacks, some 14 attacks, 13 or 14, that have been cataloged by the French Government. It is time that our governments speak out about, again, the use of chemical weapons on those civilians. Various credible sources have reported that these barrel bombs have, in fact, been filled with weaponized chlorine in recent weeks despite the regime's alleged commitment to cease all chemical weapons attacks. It is my intent to write a letter to the President asking what he is going to do about this, and I would urge any member of this committee to join me in that letter. And I welcome our esteemed panelists today, who I suspect will be able to attest to many of these challenges, especially the regime's attacks against medical personnel and facilities, and Dr. Sahloul, a close friend of the committee and president of the Syrian American Medical Society, SAMS, joins us today after recently returning from yet another trip to Syria, where he personally provided aid and witnessed unspeakable horrors. He along with others in the Syrian American community have contributed heroically to the American and international response to this humanitarian disaster. And I applaud their efforts and I encourage the administration and the U.N. to work more closely with Syrian American groups. That is where we should be moving the aid, through Syrian American groups. Frankly, if we moved all our aid through Syrian American groups, to me, that would be the ideal solution. I have communicated that to the administration. That ensures that our assistance reaches those Syrians who most need it.

Thank you very much, Madam Chair.

Ms. ROS-LEHTINEN. Thank you very much, Mr. Royce, Mr. Chairman, for joining us. It is always a delight to have you with us. Thank you.

I would like to yield for a minute opening statement at this time, Brad, if you would like.

Mr. SCHNEIDER. Thank you, Madam Chair.

I want to thank the witnesses for being here. We all know how large and significant the crisis is in Syria. I am looking forward to the testimony. I know that we need to make sure we are doing all we can to take care of the refugees, to take care of our allies in the region, and to make sure that we bring a political end and a peaceful end sooner rather than later to this crisis.

So, again, I thank you for being here.

And I will yield back.

Ms. ROS-LEHTINEN. Thank you, Mr. Schneider.

Mr. Kinzinger, if you have an opening statement for 1 minute.

Mr. KINZINGER. Well, thank you, and thank you to the panelists for being here and thank you for holding this hearing. I am just very interested in hearing obviously about the situation on the ground. I am a big believer that it is high time for the United States and the West to get involved and to ensure the overthrow of the Assad regime and to support the Free Syrian Army. So I am interested in hearing ways that we can do that but also through the humanitarian crisis ensure that everybody is taken care of. So thank you for holding this hearing, and I will yield back.

Ms. ROS-LEHTINEN. Thank you. Thank you to all the members. Now we will continue with our witnesses.

Ms. Solberg, you are recognized.

STATEMENT OF MS. HOLLY SOLBERG, DIRECTOR OF EMERGENCY AND HUMANITARIAN ASSISTANCE, CARE

Ms. SOLBERG. Chairwoman Ros-Lehtinen, Ranking Member Deutch, members of the subcommittee, thank you for holding this important hearing and for inviting me on behalf of CARE to testify before you today. My statement today is a summary of the statement I have submitted for the record.

The United Nations Under Secretary for Humanitarian Affairs and Emergency Relief, Valerie Amos, has described the crisis in and around Syria as the biggest humanitarian crisis the world today faces, with little signs of abating. I can assure you that her statement is not an exaggeration. CARE has decades of experience responding to humanitarian crises, and this is by far one of the worst we have seen. CARE works in 87 countries around the world, supporting poverty-fighting development and humanitarian assistance projects. Between 2012 and 2013, CARE responded to 53 emergencies in 34 countries, reaching over 4 million people.

In our response, we place support for the needs and rights of women and girls at the heart of our humanitarian programming. Of the close to 3 million Syrian refugees, 75 percent are women and children. I want to focus my remarks today on three areas: First, a description of what CARE has witnessed on the ground in and around Syria since the conflict began and its impacts on Syrian refugees, internally displaced people, and neighboring countries; second, CARE's response to this crisis; and, third, the important role of the United States Government.

As you know, the Syrian crisis has shattered millions of lives, the economy is in ruins. Every aspect of social and physical infrastructure has been seriously damaged with long-term erosion of livelihoods, assets, and access to education. More than 220,000 people remain trapped in besieged areas, and several million more Syrian civilians are prevented from reaching life-saving humanitarian assistance inside Syria. The high intensity of the conflict has led to new ways of large-scale displacement, both within Syria and in neighboring countries. Syria's neighbors are generously hosting almost 3 million refugees who have been forced to flee their homes, a number that is expected to rise to over 4 million by the end of this year.

This has placed an inordinate pressure on these hosting nations. For example, in Jordan, with a population of just over 6 million, is hosting nearly 600,000 refugees. The protracted nature of this conflict not only increases tensions between refugees and host communities, it also weakens the development opportunities of those displaced as well as the stability of the region. CARE's goal is to ensure the dignity and resilience of those most affected by the Syrian regional crisis so that they are empowered to support the social and economic recovery of their communities. To date, CARE and our partners have provided life-saving services to more than 400,000 people in Jordan, Lebanon, Egypt, and to the people inside Syria. Some of our intervention areas include emergency cash assistance, provision of food and other basic necessities, and psychosocial support to name a few. We have set up urban centers where refugees and vulnerable host community members can have access to available services as well as be referred to specialized external services. This approach also helps to reduce tensions between refugees and host communities. Our support to families affected by the Syrian crisis is based on humanitarian needs alone, regardless of religion, political affiliation or ethnicity. While CARE is working to scale up our response in Syria, we have so far reached more than 170,000 people, much of our focus is to assist refugees living in urban or noncamp settings because they make up the majority, approximately 80 percent, of those living in neighboring countries. In addition to our focus on urban refugees and people displaced within Syria, CARE has partnered with UNHCR and the Jordanian Government to establish the newly opened Azraq refugee camp.

I want to conclude by offering CARE's recommendations for how the U.S. Government can continue to play a leadership role in responding to this humanitarian crisis. While my testimony has focused on CARE's work in Syria's neighboring countries, we are working very hard to also support civilians inside Syria. That said, humanitarian access into Syria is significantly restricted and greatly limiting humanitarian organizations from reaching the millions in need. We ask Congress to work with the U.N. to find solutions to unfettered humanitarian access.

Lastly, CARE greatly appreciates the U.S. leadership in addressing the Syrian humanitarian crisis, providing more than $1.7 billion in humanitarian assistance to date. We also ask that the Fiscal Year 2015 proposed budget cut is respectfully restored to its critically needed funding.

Let me conclude with this: The Syrian conflict is the most catastrophic humanitarian crisis of our time. The U.S. Government and its partners have a pivotal role to play, not only in helping to bring an end to the conflict, but in saving millions of lives in the process. Thank you.

Ms. ROS-LEHTINEN. Thank you very much.

[The prepared statement of Ms. Solberg follows:]

Testimony of Holly Solberg
Director, Emergency and Humanitarian Assistance
CARE USA
House Committee on Foreign Affairs
Subcommittee on the Middle East and North Africa
The Humanitarian Crisis in Syria: Views from the Ground
May 21, 2014

Chairwoman Ros-Lehtinen, Ranking Member Deutsch, members of the subcommittee, thank you for holding this important hearing and for inviting me, on behalf of CARE, to testify before your committee today. The United Nations Under-Secretary for Human Affairs and Emergency Relief Valerie Amos has described the crisis in and around Syria as the biggest humanitarian crisis the world today faces today, tragically with little signs of abating. I can assure you that is not an exaggeration. CARE recognizes this is a protracted crisis that will affect the stability of the region for years to come.

CARE works in 87 countries around the world, supporting poverty-fighting development and humanitarian assistance projects. Between 2012 and 2013, CARE responded to 53 emergencies in 40 countries, reaching more than four million people.

In our response, we place support for the needs and rights of women and girls at the heart of our humanitarian programming. Of the over 2.5 million Syrian refugees, 75 percent are women and children.

CARE has a long history in the Middle East, beginning in 1948. CARE has been working with Palestinian, Iraqi, and now Syrian refugees in Jordan for many years.

I want to focus my remarks today on three areas:
- First, a description of what CARE has witnessed on the ground in and around Syria since the conflict began, and its impacts on Syrian refugees and host communities in neighboring countries.
- Second, CARE's response to this crisis with a particular focus on our urban refugee programming.
- Third, the important role the U.S. government plays in addressing the Syria humanitarian crisis and our recommendations for how the government must continue to help.

<u>Syria</u>

The numbers associated with the Syria crisis are staggering:
- over 9 million in need of humanitarian assistance
- over 2.5 million refugees, 75% of whom are women and children
- 6.5 million internally displaced persons

Inside Syria, more than half of the hospitals have been badly damaged or destroyed and serious basic food shortages are constant. The economy is in ruins, and thousands of schools destroyed in a country where one-third of the population is 14 years old or younger. Every aspect of social and physical infrastructure has been seriously damaged, with long-term erosion of livelihoods, assets, and access to education. More than 220,000 people remain trapped in besieged areas in Syria, and several million Syrian civilians are prevented from reaching life-saving humanitarian assistance.

The high intensity of the conflict has led to new waves of large-scale displacement, both within Syria and neighboring countries. Lebanon reached the unfortunate milestone of one million refugees last month, with Syrian refugees representing one-quarter of Lebanon's current total population.

Syrian Refugees and Host Communities

The crisis has seriously impacted Syria's regional neighbors, who are generously hosting more than 2.5 million women, men, and children who have fled their homes. This has placed an inordinate pressure on these hosting nations and host communities. Jordan, with a population of just over six million, is housing nearly 600,000 Syrian refugees. To put this in context, this would be equivalent to the United States taking in more than 30 million refugees.

According to the United Nations High Commissioner for Refugees (UNHCR), this figure is expected to rise to 4.1 million by the end of 2014. The protracted nature of this conflict means that sadly the challenges they face will grow, threatening their stability as well as the stability of the region.

Host countries and local communities face significant difficulties coping with the impact of the crisis on public services. Critical shortages of shelter and a lack of income-generating opportunities further strain living conditions, with many Syrian refugees forced to live in inadequate make-shift shelters. An increasing number of Syrian refugees are at risk of eviction due to their inability to afford rent.

In April 2014, CARE issued a report: *Hidden Lives: Urban Syrian Refugees and Jordanian Host Communities Three Years into the Syria Crisis.* A key concern highlighted in this report was that Syrian refugees will continue to depend on humanitarian assistance while awaiting return, three years into the displacement crisis, all actors involved in the response must increasingly diversify their programming with the aim of bringing vulnerable Jordanian and Syrian families closer together. Programming includes community-support activities, strengthening the capacities of local service providers, and creating income-generating activities to reduce the tension and feeling that refugees and local vulnerable communities compete over resources and access to services.

The report also highlights the need to improve access to education for Syrian refugee families in Jordan. Despite considerable efforts, Jordanian schools struggle to accommodate the large numbers of Syrian boys and girls. According to the study, nearly half (43%) of Syrian school-aged children are out of school. In some areas, that figure is significantly higher – in Mufraq, 90% of Syrian teenage boys and girls do not attend school. To prevent the loss of an entire generation of children, much greater support is urgently needed to ensure educational opportunities for Syrian refugees. Barriers preventing children from attending school include costs associated with education, threats of harassment, economic need for children to work, different educational systems and lack of capacities in local schools. With overcrowded classrooms in Jordan, it is critical to continue to invest in the Jordanian educational system to ensure it has the capacities to accommodate Syrian school-aged children.

CARE's response

CARE's vision is to ensure the dignity and resilience of those most affected by the Syrian regional crisis, so that they are empowered to support the social and economic recovery of their communities. CARE is providing life-saving services in Jordan, Lebanon, Egypt, and also to people inside Syria. We are also undertaking initial activities in Turkey to support the increasing number of refugees in the country. To date, CARE has reached more than 400,000 people affected by the crisis through interventions, such as cash assistance, shelter, hygiene and sanitation, medical assistance, food aid, psychosocial support, prevention of gender-based violence and information services.

Our support to families affected by the crisis in Syria is based on humanitarian needs alone, regardless of their religion, political affiliation or ethnicity. As I've noted, women and children make up the majority of refugees, and are particularly vulnerable. CARE is working to address those needs by assuring they have access to basic services and safe spaces to gather and receive support.

Inside Syria, CARE's partners have provided life-saving emergency assistance to more than 170,000 people affected by the conflict. Working in close collaboration with local and diaspora Syrian groups, we are providing food and emergency supplies to families, and emergency medical equipment and support for women.

In Jordan, CARE has reached more than 250,000 refugees from Syria. CARE focuses primarily on supporting refugees in urban areas of Jordan, who often live in overcrowded apartments, many sleeping on floors with mattresses, or blankets. CARE set up and is operating urban refugee centers in Amman and three other areas (Zarqa, Irbid, and Mafraq). CARE volunteers, who are refugees themselves, assist in organizing and preparing distributions of relief supplies. We also provide cash assistance to help them pay for basic living costs. Most refugees use this support to pay for rent (50%), medication (26%) and food (17%).

Serving as a central referral system, CARE also assists newly arrived refugees in neighboring countries who often arrive with nothing more than the clothes on their back. We provide information on how they can access health, education, and social support services. In addition, we are providing psychosocial assistance to women, men, and children to help them cope with the experience of violence, flight, and loss of family and friends.

In addition to operating the urban refugee centers, CARE has partnered with UNHCR, the Jordanian government, and other agencies to set up a new refugee camp in Azraq, Jordan's sixth Syrian refugee camp. The Azraq camp was officially opened on April 30, 2014, to accommodate the continued influx of refugees from Syria with an initial capacity of 51,000. The camp could be expanded to host up to 130,000 refugees if needed. With the Za'atari refugee camp already at capacity, accommodating over 100,000 refugees, Azraq will play an important role in hosting additional refugees from Syria. Azraq is designed as four refugee 'villages', with each village hosting 10,000 to 15,000 people. Each village has its own community center, primary health center, safe spaces, recreational grounds, and schools.

Similar to our work in urban refugee centers, in Azraq, CARE plays a crucial role in providing vital information to refugees upon their arrival through community centers. These community centers inside the camp provide a safe haven for vulnerable refugees, including women, as they will be able to receive psychosocial support, engage in recreational activities, and learn new skills. We are also running various community-based activities and setting up committees of refugee representatives so that their own concerns and views are considered and community leaders are part of the decision making process within the camp setting.

Role of the United States Government

I want to conclude by offering CARE's recommendations for how the U.S. government can continue to play a leadership role in responding to this humanitarian crisis.

First, we seek unfettered humanitarian access to Syria. As you probably noted, my testimony focused on CARE's work in Syria's *neighboring* countries. Humanitarian access in Syria is significantly restricted and prohibits humanitarian organizations from reaching the millions of people in need. With limited access, and through partners, CARE has reached more than 170,000 beneficiaries inside Syria with life-saving assistance. But with improved access, CARE and our partners are poised to reach millions more. There are an estimated 9.5 million people living in Syria in need of assistance.

While we recognize and continue to call for a political resolution to the conflict, we must do all that we can now to address the devastating humanitarian crisis in the region and support the millions of vulnerable civilians affected by the conflict.

While there is high expectation in the NGO community that access will improve, unfortunately ninety days after the adoption of the U.N. Security Council passed Resolution 2139, access to and within Syria remains extremely challenging for aid agencies. CARE appreciates this committee's attention to the issue of humanitarian access outlined in H. Res. 520, a resolution calling for the immediate and full implementation of the U.N Security Council Resolution 2139, which both Chairwoman Ros-Lehtinen and Ranking Member Deutsch both cosponsored.

Lastly, CARE greatly appreciates the United States leadership in addressing the Syria humanitarian crisis, providing more than $1.7 billion in humanitarian assistance to-date. Unfortunately, despite this generosity, increased funding is desperately needed as the crisis shows no signs of waning. Three plus years into this protracted crisis, the U.S. and other donors must support both life-saving humanitarian assistance now, but also long-term funding to rebuild lives and livelihoods.

We recognize the fiscal constraints our nation faces, but are concerned that the Administration's FY 2015 budget request cut humanitarian assistance by 25%. We encourage Congress to restore this critically needed humanitarian funding as it crafts its FY 2015 State and Foreign Operations bill. To adequately address the Syria humanitarian crisis and others around the globe, it is critical this funding is restored. Stability in the Middle East is in everyone's best interest, but I would be remiss in not highlighting for this committee that as we sit here, CARE and our partners are currently addressing the other major humanitarian crisis in the world today, including South Sudan and the Central African Republic.

Thank you again for the opportunity to share CARE's experience on the ground. Let me conclude with this: the Syrian conflict is the most catastrophic humanitarian crisis of our time, and it's not going away. The U.S. government and its partners have a pivotal role to play, not only in helping to bring an end to the conflict, but in saving millions of lives in the process. Thank you.

Ms. Ros-Lehtinen. Ms. Wanek.

STATEMENT OF MS. PIA WANEK, DIRECTOR, OFFICE OF HUMANITARIAN ASSISTANCE, GLOBAL COMMUNITIES

Ms. Wanek. Chairwoman Ros-Lehtinen, Ranking Member Deutch, members of the committee, thank you for the opportunity to testify today on the important topic of the Syrian refugee crisis. I will present to you now an abridged version of our written testimony.

I am the director of humanitarian assistance for Global Communities. Global Communities is working in Lebanon in partnership with UNHCR to assist Syrian refugees and Lebanese host communities. Our organization has worked in Lebanon since 1997 through many conflicts and disastrous situations. This crisis, however, is of a scale, new scale altogether. In April 2014, the number of Syrian refugees in Lebanon exceeded 1 million, nearly 40 percent of the total Syrian refugee population in the region. Among this million are more than 300,000 unschooled children working or begging in the streets. Syrian refugees in Lebanon constitute 20 percent of the total population of the country. This is as though the entire population of Canada was uprooted and moved into the USA twice. There is no other country in the world today that hosts such a high proportion of refugees compared to its own citizens. My remarks today will address the situation in Lebanon specifically along two main points.

My first point: Syrian refugees and Lebanese citizens are competing against each other for the same resources. We must increasingly focus our support on longer-term solutions for host communities and Syrian refugees, as shared services have reached a breaking point. Before the Syrian war, Lebanese communities across the country were already poor, with 23 percent living below the poverty line. The influx of refugees has exacerbated the situation. With the bulk of assistance going to refugees, Lebanese communities are worse off than ever. The World Bank estimates an additional 170,000 Lebanese have been pushed into poverty by the crisis and that, by the end of 2014, 75 percent of Lebanon's 4.1 million citizens will be in need of some form of financial shelter or food support.

With the refugee crisis accelerating, we must consider the situation in Lebanon to be longer term. We must position the aid that is being supplied so that we are providing durable solutions for the needs of the refugees and their Lebanese hosts. This goes beyond shelter, food, and medicine into providing assistance to reduce the strain on Lebanon's shared housing, energy, education, and water resources.

This leads to my second point. Failure to support refugees and host communities will create a destabilizing effect in Lebanon and throughout the region. The more than 300,000 unschooled Syrian refugee children are vulnerable to recruitment by radical groups. Disenfranchised Lebanese youth are also vulnerable to such recruitment. Where there are gaps in refugee and host community assistance, extremist factions are stepping in and exploiting vulnerable populations. Our experience on the ground is that Lebanese community members are reporting an increase in disputes relating to Syrian refugees. Law enforcement officials believe an increase in the crime rate is linked with the growth of the Syrian population, and whether these claims are rumor or fact is difficult to determine, but the perception alone is damaging enough to relations between Syrian and Lebanese communities. Syrian refugees will be in Lebanon for many years to come. Aid needs to be focused on easing the divide between communities, identifying common interests, and creating shared benefits. Failure to do so will allow simmering tensions to escalate and destabilize a country already deeply vulnerable to conflict. There is a tremendous danger of the Syrian conflict erupting in Lebanon and then spiraling outwards into a regional conflict, engulfing U.S. allies, such as Israel and Jordan.

In December 2013, UNHCR released projected funding needs for 2014. The plan appealed for $4.2 billion to cover assistance to refugees and host communities across the region. It is the largest donor pledge in history. The total U.S. humanitarian commitment is more than $1.7 billion, the largest of any nation. Nevertheless, the appeal is only 25 percent funded. Unfilled, there is not enough assistance for refugees or host communities. We recommend that the U.S. Government continue to support the needs, immediate and longer term, of the people affected by this conflict. We strongly encourage the U.S. Government and other governments to live up to their pledges to ensure that the response to the crisis is fully funded. We recommend that the United States Congress in particular provide robust funding for the humanitarian assistance accounts of the Fiscal Year 2015 Federal budget as detailed in our written testimony. We commend the U.S. Government for its leadership and commitment to protecting the vulnerable communities around the Syrian conflict. We ask that you continue to provide this support as an example to the international community. Thank you.

Ms. ROS-LEHTINEN. Thank you very much, Ms. Wanek.

[The prepared statement of Ms. Wanek follows:]

Global Communities
Partners for Good

"The Humanitarian Crisis in Syria: Views from the Ground"

Testimony by
Pia Wanek
Director, Office of Humanitarian Assistance, Global Communities

Before the
House Committee on Foreign Affairs
Subcommittee on Middle East and North Africa
May 21, 2014

Chairwoman Ros-Lehtinen, Ranking Member Deutsch, Members of the Committee, thank you for the opportunity to testify today on the important topic of the Syrian refugee crisis.

I am the Director of Humanitarian Assistance for Global Communities. Global Communities is working in Lebanon in partnership with UNHCR to implement shelter and infrastructure assistance programs, such as repairing homes and schools for Syrian refugees and Lebanese host communities in Beirut and Mt. Lebanon, a district located approximately 30 minutes from downtown Beirut. Our organization has been working in Lebanon since 1997 and we have worked through many conflicts and disaster situations, including the 2006 war. This crisis, however, is of a new scale altogether[1].

The number of Syrian refugees today exceeds 2.7 million and continues to grow rapidly. Women and children make up 75% of the refugees. In April 2014, the number of Syrian refugees in Lebanon alone exceeded one million, nearly 40% of the total refugee population. Among this million in Lebanon are more than 300,000 unschooled children working or begging in the streets, vulnerable to labor and sexual exploitation.

To give you some sense of scale of the crisis, the one million Syrian refugees in Lebanon constitute at least 20% of the total population of the country. This is as though the entire population of Canada was uprooted and moved into the USA – twice over. But in area, Lebanon is only one-third of the size of the state of Maryland. Without understanding this sense of scale it is hard to comprehend the density of population, the stress on resources and the escalating tensions and hostilities between Syrian refugees and their Lebanese hosts. The country is like a pressure cooker ready to explode. There is no other country in the world today that hosts such a high proportion of refugees compared to its own citizens, and that number will only increase as the war continues to rage across the border in Syria.

---

[1] "Syrian Refugee Crisis: Rapid Needs Assessment in Lebanon" Global Communities, May 14, 2014
http://www.globalcommunities.org/node/37816

The Lebanese government should be commended for continuing to keep its borders open. To date, Lebanon has been welcoming and supportive to Syrians throughout the conflict, but that welcome is wearing thin. The sense of fatigue in supporting the crisis is everywhere—from the refugees themselves to the Lebanese community members and the aid actors attempting to provide support. Today Lebanon is facing a breaking point in its capacity to absorb any more refugees.

My remarks today will address the situation in Lebanon specifically, along two main points.

1 – Syrian refugees and Lebanese citizens are competing against each other for the same water, energy and economic resources. We must increasingly focus our support on medium-to-long term solutions for host communities and Syrian refugees, as these shared services have reached a breaking point.

2 – The failure to support refugees and host communities will likely create a destabilizing effect in Lebanon that will reverberate throughout the region.

1 – Syrian refugees and Lebanese citizens are competing against each other for the same water, energy and economic resources. We must increasingly focus our support on medium-to-long term solutions for host communities and Syrian refugees, as these shared services have reached a breaking point.

Pre-dating the Syrian war, Lebanese communities across the country were already poor and vulnerable with 23% living below the poverty line of $4 a day. Most refugees are living in 242 locations in Lebanon which were classified as the most vulnerable and poor in the country, even before the presence of the refugees. The influx of refugees has only worsened the situation and strained shared public services to the breaking point. However, the bulk of assistance has gone to refugees, leaving Lebanese communities worse off than ever. The World Bank estimates an additional 170,000 Lebanese have been pushed into poverty since the start of the Syrian crisis and that by the end of 2014, 3.15 million of Lebanon's 4.1 million citizens will be in need of some form of financial, shelter or food support.[2] For example:

- Prices of basic commodities, food, and transportation have increased with growing demand, while intense labor competition has driven wages downwards. Rental prices for even the most basic shelters in many areas have increased two to three-fold as Lebanese landlords have been taking advantage of the demand-driven market.
- Access to reliable water sources is a critical issue. Problems with water quality, supply and inadequate sanitation services that pre-date the Syrian crisis continue to deteriorate in Lebanon[3]. Additionally, reports indicate a decrease in 54% from the general average in rainfall over the past 30 years, drastically exacerbating the supply problem.

UNHCR defines a protracted refugee situation as at least 25,000 refugees seeking asylum in a country for at least five years. Resolving protracted situations requires at least one of the three durable solutions for refugees: voluntary return to their home countries in safety and dignity; local

---

[2] http://www.worldbank.org/en/news/feature/2013/09/24/lebanon-bears-the-brunt-of-the-economic-and-social-spillovers-of-the-syrian-conflict

[3] National Water Sector Strategy, Ministry of Energy and Water, March 2012.

integration in their country of asylum; or third-country resettlement[4]. With the Syrian refugee crisis accelerating and with no end in sight of the war that precipitates it, we must consider the situation in Lebanon to be a long-term, protracted situation. We must position the aid that is being supplied so that we are considering durable, long-term solutions for the needs of refugees and their Lebanese hosts. This goes beyond shelter, food, medicine and essential items into providing assistance to host communities to reduce the strain on Lebanon's shared housing, energy, education and water sources.

2- The failure to support refugees and host communities will create a destabilizing effect in Lebanon and reverberate throughout the region

Global Communities believes that we should support refugees and host communities according to the humanitarian imperative that action should always be taken to prevent or alleviate human suffering arising out of disaster or conflict. These people are fleeing terrible violence and are living in hazardous conditions with little security in countries that may or may not welcome their presence. There are also practical reasons for continuing this support:

- More than 300,000 unschooled Syrian refugee children, including 2,440 refugee children with parental support or supervision[5], are vulnerable to labor and sexual exploitation, and they are also vulnerable to recruitment by radical groups. The growing number of disenfranchised youth in host communities are also vulnerable to radical ideology and recruitment into extremist groups.
- Where there is a failure to aid the Lebanese government in the provision of refugee and host community assistance, extremist factions have stepped into the gap and exploited vulnerable populations. A generation of disenfranchised young people can lead to terrible long-term consequences.
- Our experience on the ground is that Lebanese community members report both verbal and physical altercations between residents as well as an uptick in disputes, discrimination and harassment. Lebanese often express concern with the increasing number of Syrians and associate them with anti-social behavior including delinquent youth, harassment and violence against women. Law enforcement officials believe an increase in the crime rate is linked with the growth of the Syrian population. Whether these claims are rumor or fact is often difficult to determine, but the perception is damaging enough to relations between Lebanese communities and reflects the growing tensions.

The harsh reality is that the Syrians will be in Lebanon for the medium term, at the very least. Aid needs to be focused on easing the divide between communities, identifying common interests and creating shared benefits. Failure to do so will allow simmering tensions to reach unsustainable levels that could easily destabilize a country already deeply vulnerable to conflict with a tenuous political and fragile sectarian balance. There is a tremendous danger of the Syrian conflict erupting in Lebanon and then spiraling outwards into a regional conflict, engulfing U.S. allies such as Israel and Jordan. This is a grave situation to be avoided at all costs.

[4] US Department of State. http://www.state.gov/j/prm/policyissues/issues/protracted/#1
[5] UNHCR. The Future of Syria. Refugee Children in Crisis. http://unhcr.org/FutureOfSyria/executive-summary.html#syrian-refugee-children

Future Steps in Resolving the Humanitarian Crisis

In December 2013, UNHCR released the sixth iteration of the Syria Regional Response Plan, a united effort on behalf of international aid providers in the region to present a consolidated number of projected funding needs for 2014. The Plan appealed for $4.2 billion to cover the needs of the 4.1 million refugees expected to flee Syria and 2.7 million people in host communities by the end of December 2014[6]. It is the largest donor pledge in history and will likely remain underfunded due to limited funds allocated for humanitarian assistance and the growing sense of donor fatigue.

At the Humanitarian Pledging Conference for Syria in Kuwait on January 15, 2014, Secretary of State John Kerry announced that the US would contribute an additional $380 million to Syrian humanitarian efforts—bringing the total US humanitarian commitment to more than $1.7 billion, the largest of any nation[7]. Nevertheless, the appeal is only 25% funded.[8]

Unfilled, there is not enough assistance for refugees and host communities.

- We recommend that the U.S. Government continue to support the needs of the victims of this conflict for both emergency aid and development of Lebanese communities in response to the protracted nature of this conflict. We strongly encourage the U.S. Government and other governments to live up to their pledges to ensure that the response to the crisis is fully funded. Refugees and host communities must both be supported, for both humanitarian and security reasons linked to the potential broader destabilization of the region.
- We recommend that the United States Congress in particular provide robust funding for the humanitarian assistance accounts of the FY15 federal budget. The humanitarian community was concerned to see a 25% cut to these accounts in the President's request. In order for us to be able to respond to this and other crises around the world, we request the following amounts:
  - International Disaster Assistance - $2.1 billion
  - Migration and Refugee Assistance - $3.1 billion
  - Food for Peace - $1.866 billion

We commend the U.S. Government for its moral leadership and financial commitment to protecting the vulnerable communities around the Syrian conflict. We ask that you continue to provide this support and to be an example to the wider world.

---

[6] http://www.unhcr.org/syriarrp6/
[7] http://www.state.gov/r/pa/prs/ps/2014/01/220029.htm
[8] http://www.unocha.org/crisis/syria

Ms. Ros-Lehtinen. Dr. Sahloul.

STATEMENT OF ZAHER SAHLOUL, M.D., PRESIDENT, SYRIAN AMERICAN MEDICAL SOCIETY

Dr. Sahloul. Good afternoon. Thank you, Chairman Ros-Lehtinen and Ranking Member Mr. Deutch for sponsoring this and for inviting me.

Thank you for my friend Mr. Schneider, we worked in Chicago for interfaith dialogue with the Catholic Theological Union, and we are here today on a different occasion.

And thank you for Mr. Kinzinger, who worked closely with the Syrian American community in Illinois also.

To me, it is very personal because I am the only Syrian American on this panel. I have family in Syria, and as you have mentioned, I have gone several times to Syria as a medical mission to make sure that our friends, our colleagues, the Syrian American physicians and nurses have what they need in terms of medical supplies and medications and equipment. And I can tell you that with the help of our Government, SAMS and other Syrian American organizations are able to get any medical equipment or medical supplies or medication to any place in Syria across the border, and we would like to urge our Government to support expansion of these cross-border operations because we think that this is the only thing that can save millions of people from illness or from food shortages.

I can tell you also that by the end of this hearing, unfortunately, we will have 800 more Syrians who are displaced, among them 600 women and children and among them 400 children who will not have education. By the end of this hearing, also, we will have another 200 people in Syria who are killed. By the end of this hearing, we will have 500 more people in Syria who have lifelong disability. We are talking about a scale of disaster that is unencountered in our life. This is the worst disaster that you will have in your life. The number of people impacted in Syria by the crisis by the disaster are more than the total number combined of the disaster in South Sudan and Central African Republic, in Bosnia, and Rwanda combined. We are talking about the worst humanitarian disaster in our time.

I came recently from Syria. I am a critical care specialist. I go there and take care of patients in the ICU, and I brought some pictures, so I hope that you can bear with me in looking at these pictures. I want to first mention some of the stories that I have encountered. The first one is about a child, his name is Mohamad Alabrash. He was preparing to go to school. He is 6 years old. And then he heard the sound of helicopter. He looked at the sky, and then the helicopter threw a barrel bomb. Then he saw yellow smoke coming out, and then he started choking, him and his mother, who was pregnant, also. They started choking, and they have respiratory symptoms, and they were taken to the emergency room of a field hospital where they had to be intubated because they had fluid in their lungs, they had respiratory failure. They were transported to a border hospital that were supplied by ventilators and monitored by our organization. Unfortunately, the child, Mohamad Alabrash, has died; his mother, who was pregnant, was saved. This happened in April 21st, only a few weeks ago.

Yesterday, there was another chemical weapons attack in the City of Kafr Zita north of Hama, and one person who is 14 years old with special needs died, another person who is 70 years old also has died. Most of the people who were exposed to chemical weapons attacks in the last few months were civilians. According to our report that we combined in the field, 1,000 people had symptoms related to exposure to chemical agents. Among them, 12 people who were killed because of exposure to chemical agents. This is not sarin gas. This is not nerve gas. This is what is called a choking agent. It is called chlorine gas according to our experts in the field.

We urge President Obama to use all of his powers to stop the chemical weapon attacks on Syrians and also to stop the barrel bombing attacks on the City of Aleppo. Two things that are hurting Syrian civilians more at this point, chemical weapon attacks and barrel bombing attacks. In the City of Aleppo, I went there in October and the streets were bustling with people and civilians. Right now, 75 percent of the people in the City of Aleppo have deserted this place because of the barrel bombing campaign that started in December of last year. I have seen hospitals that were bombed. I have seen schools that were bombed. I have seen neighborhoods that were full of people that right now are ghost towns. And I have seen physicians and nurses, you know, struggling to save their patients, and they are asking for all kinds of assistance. One of the physicians in one of the hospitals told me, Please send us everything that you can, antibiotics, gloves, and also send us body bags because we run out of body bags.

I believe that our Nation is able to do much more than what we have done in the past. I urge you to support humanitarian assistance to the Syrians, but I urge you also to do much more to end the crisis and force a political settlement. Thank you.

Ms. Ros-Lehtinen. Thank you very much, Doctor. Thank you for your work.

[The prepared statement of Dr. Sahloul follows:]

The Humanitarian Crisis in Syria: Views from the Ground

Testimony by Dr. Zaher Sahloul, President of the Syrian American Medical Society (SAMS), to the House Foreign Relations Committee, Subcommittee on the Middle East and North Africa. May 21, 2014.

Introduction

On behalf of SAMS, I would like to thank you all for this opportunity to testify about our experiences providing medical relief inside Syria and the relevant lessons we have learned. I would like to thank Chairman Rep. Edward Royce for inviting me to testify at this committee and for sponsoring House Resolution 520, demanding expanded humanitarian access and an end to attacks on civilians. I strongly urge the House of Representatives to pass this resolution.

Additionally, I commend Chairwoman Rep. Ileana Ros-Lehtinen for her strong condemnation of chemical weapons attacks in Syria, and commend Ranking Member Rep. Theodore E. Deutch for his demonstrated commitment to stopping the flow of weapons into Syria.

SAMS recognizes Rep. Brad Schneider for being a supportive friend in this crisis and recognizes Illinois Rep. Adam Kinzinger, who has worked closely with SAMS to develop proactive policy to end the Syrian crisis.

Furthermore, I would like to thank all members of the Subcommittee on the Middle East and North Africa for their continued support for the provision of humanitarian assistance to Syria.

Executive Summary:

SAMS is a leading Syrian American Diaspora NGO providing cross-border medical relief to Syria from our offices in Turkey and Jordan. SAMS's programs focus on addressing the direct and indirect consequences of the Syrian crisis. Thanks to our generous donors, SAMS supports field and trauma hospitals, training courses for physicians, fuel and generators for hospitals, medical equipment and supplies, medical staff salaries, and rebuilding of hospitals destroyed by bombing.

Despite all of our efforts, the humanitarian situation in Syria continues to deteriorate. As barrel bombs rain on Syria's cities, millions of Syrians have fled their homes for safety elsewhere. According the UN, 6.5 million Syrians are internally displaced and 2.7 million Syrians are living as refugees in neighboring countries. Much of the country's infrastructure has been destroyed, the economy is in shambles, food insecurity is rising, and the social and communal bonds between Syrians continue to degrade into sectarianism.

Worse, chemical weapons attacks against Syrian civilians continue. Chlorine gas attacks in northern Syria last month left 5 dead and 1000 in need of treatment.[1] These attacks are designed to terrorize local populations into submission or flight, compelling Syrians to seek refuge abroad before their villages are targeted. Chemical weapons attacks also act as an impediment to the efficiency of our operations, channeling our already-limited resources to chemical weapons programs instead of conventional trauma and primary care.

SAMS calls for the following:

1.   The president should end barrel bombing and chemical weapons attacks by any means necessary.
2.   Congress should increase funding for humanitarian assistance to the Syrian people to match expected increased need. This aid should be redirected to reach Syrian populations along the Turkish, Jordanian, and Lebanese borders that are inaccessible through cross-line or official humanitarian assistance operations.
3.   The US government should provide training and financial support to healthcare workers operating inside Syria to encourage them to remain in the country in the face of the collapsing healthcare system.
4.   The US government should rebalance funding to Syrian and Syrian diaspora NGOs as such organizations have strong connections with local NGOs, help empower non-violent Syrian civil society, understand local needs, and counteract the influence of extremist groups.
5.   The US should pressure the UN Office for the Coordination of Humanitarian Affairs (UNOCHA) to provide direct assistance to local and diaspora NGOs for cross-border relief efforts. The US should also pressure UNOCHA to expedite its coordination of humanitarian assistance across the border.

---

[1] CBRNTF. Report on Toxic Gas Attacks in the Suburbs of Idlib and Hama. Rep. Chemical, Biological, Radiological and Nuclear Task Force, 15 May 2014. Web. 19 May 2014. <http://goo.gl/qKdOKI>.

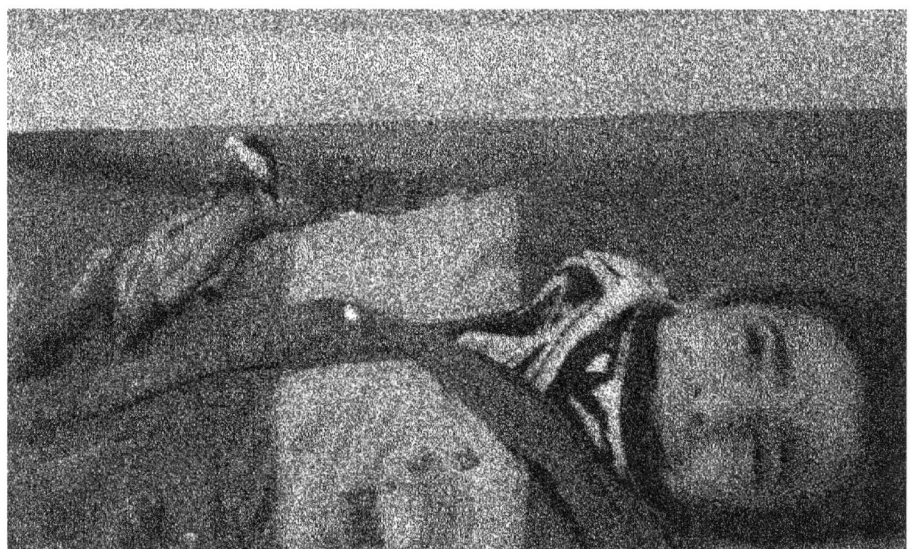

A child in the emergency room of a SAMS supported hospital who was a victim of a barrel bombing attack in a civilian neighborhood in Aleppo.

A Devastating Toll:

The ongoing armed conflict in Syria has entered its fourth year unabated. It is estimated that more than 150,000 people have been killed, among them 11,420 children.[2] 11,000 prisoners have been tortured to death,[3] and at least 1,400 people died from suffocation due to exposure to Sarin nerve gas and other internationally prohibited chemical agents.[4]

According to UNOCHA, more than 9.3 million Syrians, or close to half of the population, are in need of assistance and that number is increasing every day. According to UNICEF, 1.2 million children have become refugees and another 3 million children are internally displaced within Syria.[5] Approximately 2.8 million children lack consistent access to education, resulting in a lost generation of Syrian youth.[6] Currently, more than 2.7 million Syrians are registered as refugees

[2]"Press Release: Major New Report Shows 11,420 Children Killed in Syrian Conflict: 7 out of 10 by Explosives, 1 in 4 by Bullets | Oxford Research Group." Press Release: Major New Report Shows 11,420 Children Killed in Syrian Conflict: 7 out of 10 by Explosives, 1 in 4 by Bullets | Oxford Research Group. Web. 19 May 2014.
<http://www.oxfordresearchgroup.org.uk/publications/middle_east/press_release_new_report_stolen_futures_hidden_death_toll_child_casualties_>.

[3]Ibid.

[4]Warrick,Joby. " More than 1,400 killed in Syrian chemical weapons attack, U.S.Says." *The Washington Post.* 30 August 2013.
<http://www.washingtonpost.com/world/national-security/nearly-1500-killed-in-syrian-chemical-weapons-attack-us-says/2013/08/30/b2864662-1196-11e3-85b6-d27422650fd5_story.html>

[5] UNICEF. " Under Siege/ The devastating impact on children of three years of conflict in Syria".:
<http://www.unicef.org/publications/files/Under_Siege_March_2014.pdf>

[6] "Syria is one of the most dangerous places in the world to be a child." *UNICEF United States Fund.*
<http://www.unicefusa.org/mission/emergencies/conflict/syria>

by the UNHCR in neighboring countries and at least 6.5 million are internally displaced.[7] Every day, 9,500 more Syrians are forced to flee.[8] In Lebanon, one out of three people is a Syrian refugee.[9] In Jordan, the Al-Zaatari camp is now the country's fourth largest city and the second largest refugee camp in the world.[10] This year, Syria will replace Afghanistan as the nation with the highest refugee population in the world.[11]

The Impact of the Syrian Crisis on the Public Healthcare System:

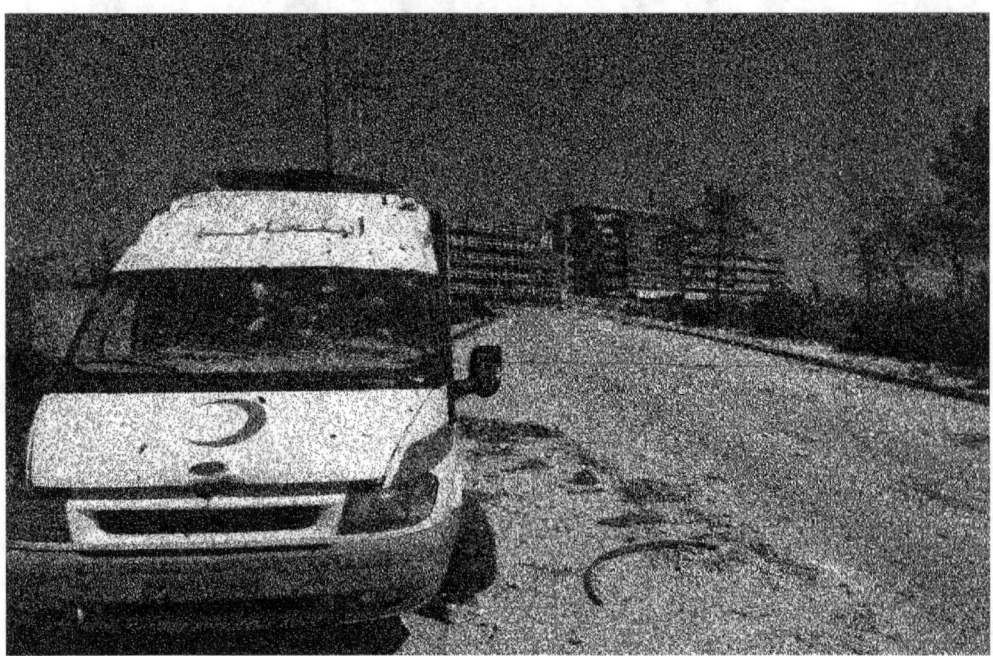

The Al-Kindi Medical Campus north of Aleppo after it was completely destroyed

The ongoing conflict has devastated the country's healthcare system. The Geneva Convention prohibits warring parties from attacking doctors, ambulances, or hospitals displaying a Red Cross or Red Crescent emblems; such targeting is considered a war crime. In Syria, no such

---

[7] The United Nations Refugee Agency " Syria Regional Response Plan." http://data.unhcr.org/syrianrefugees/regional.php>

[8] "UN-backed report reveals record 33.3 million people displaced by war last year." *UN News Center.* 14 May 2014.<http://www.un.org/apps/news/story.asp?NewsID=47787#.U3pBGfldVlo>

[9] Hubbard, Be. " Lebanon Hosts Over a Million who fled Syria, UN Reports." The New York Times. Web. 3 April, 2014. <http://www.nytimes.com/2014/04/04/world/middleeast/syrian-refugees-one-million.html>

[10] "UNHCR - Refugees Daily." *UNHCR - Refugees Daily.* Web. 19 May 2014. <http://www.unhcr.org/cgi-bin/texis/vtx/refdaily?pass=463ef21123&id=5372fee98>.

[11] Nichols, Michelle. "Syrians Set to Replace Afghans as Largest Refugee Population: U.N." *Reuters.* Thomson Reuters, 25 Feb. 2014. Web. 19 May 2014. <http://www.reuters.com/article/2014/02/25/us-syria-crisis-un-idUSBREA1O1MA20140225>.

norms or conventions are respected. Instead, healthcare professionals, hospitals and ambulances have been systematically targeted since the beginning of the crisis.

According to the World Health Organization (WHO), only 27% of hospitals in Syria appeared to be fully functioning due to the destruction of facilities and a lack of staff, equipment, and medicine.[12] More than 460 healthcare workers have been killed.[13] More than 15,000 physicians have fled to other countries.[14] In Aleppo, a city of more than 2.5 million people, only 300 physicians remained, including only 16 surgeons and 3 Orthopedic surgeons.[15] Rescue workers have also been targeted. The Syrian Red Crescent has lost at least 34 volunteers killed in the line of duty while transporting patients or delivering humanitarian supplies.[16]

Key metrics, such as rates of access to safe and affordable healthcare, vaccinations, neonatal mortality, maternal mortality, and women's health benchmarks have all plummeted as a result of the conflict. The WHO has confirmed the resurgence of infectious diseases like Polio and Leishmaniasis and the emergence of epidemics of Measles, Typhoid, Hepatitis, H1N1 and Tuberculosis. SAMS estimates that at least 200,000 civilians have died due to non-communicable chronic diseases (NCD)[17] such as untreated cancer and renal failure.

---

[12] " World Health Organization Fact Sheet, The Syrian Arab Republic." *World Health Organization*. Web. <http://www.who.int/hac/crises/syr/sitreps/syria_country_fact_sheet_13march2014_final.pdf?ua=1>

[13]"Physicians for Human Rights." - *New Map Shows Government Forces Deliberately Attacking Syria's Medical System*. Web. 19 May 2014. <http://physiciansforhumanrights.org/press/press-releases/new-map-shows-government-forces-deliberately-attacking-syrias-medical-system.html>.

[14] "Syria's Medical Community Under Assault." - *Syria's Medical Community Under Assault*. Physicians for Human Rights, May 2014. Web. 19 May 2014. <https://s3.amazonaws.com/PHR_other/Syria%27s-Medical-Community-Under-Assault-May-2014.pdf>.

[15] *Ibid*.

[16] *Ibid*.

[17] Murugen, Jerusha. "Syria's Other Crisis." *CNN*. Fareed Zakaria GPS, 30 Sept. 2013. Web. 19 May 2014. <http://globalpublicsquare.blogs.cnn.com/2013/09/30/syrias-other-crisis/>.

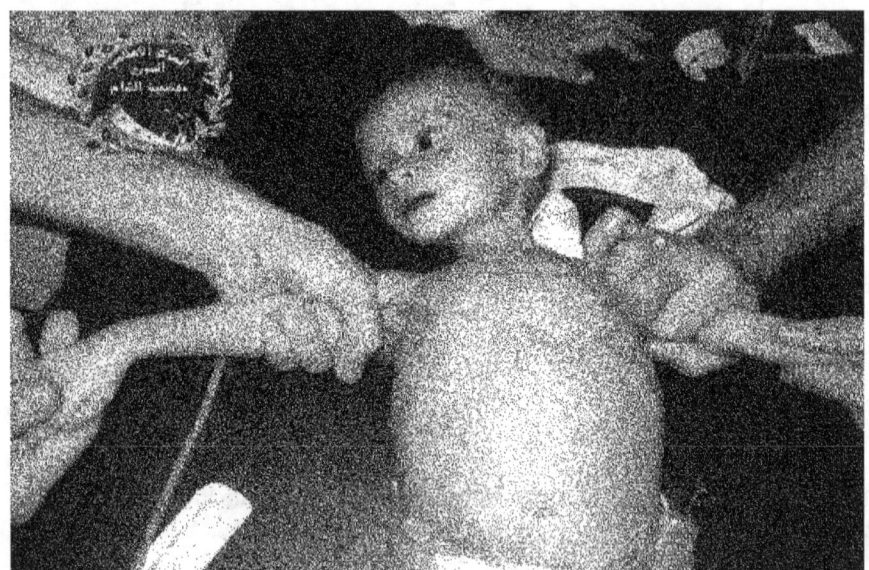

Syrian child with severe malnutrition due to the siege of Moaddameyya district near Damascus

SAMS and other Syrian Diaspora NGOs are struggling to provide lifesaving medical and humanitarian relief that targets populations that are inaccessible to UN agencies. SAMS prioritizes addressing the needs of patients and healthcare workers inside Syria and in neighboring countries. We strive to abide by the humanitarian principles of medical neutrality, impartiality, and independence, and to follow best practices in humanitarian and nonprofit operations.

An emergency room in a SAMS supported hospital that was partially destroyed by guided missile, is fortified for the next barrel bomb with IV fluid, Ambu Bags, defibrillators, and sand bags.

The International Response to the Syrian Humanitarian Crisis: Reactive, Disconnected, and Inadequate

Thus far, the response of the international community has been woefully inadequate to meet the needs of the Syrian people. The UN and many international NGOs have issued multiple reports addressing the numerous aspects of the crisis, while failing to provide practical, proactive and sustainable solutions. The United Nations Security Council (UNSC) has neglected to address the needs of the estimated 242,000 Syrians living in besieged areas inside Syria.[18] Most aid

---

[18] *Humanitarian Bulletin Syrian Arab Republic.* Rep. Issue. 44. UN OCHA. Web.19 May 2014.
<http://reliefweb.int/sites/reliefweb.int/files/resources/Syria%20Humanitarian%20Bulletin%2044.pdf>

provided through the United Nations Response Plan has been directed to areas under Syrian Government control, neglecting Syrians in need of assistance who are living in opposition-held areas. Recent reports show that at least 85% of food aid and 70% of medicine aid provided through UN agencies were sent to areas controlled by the Syrian government, compared to 50% of aid distributed by the UN last year.[19]

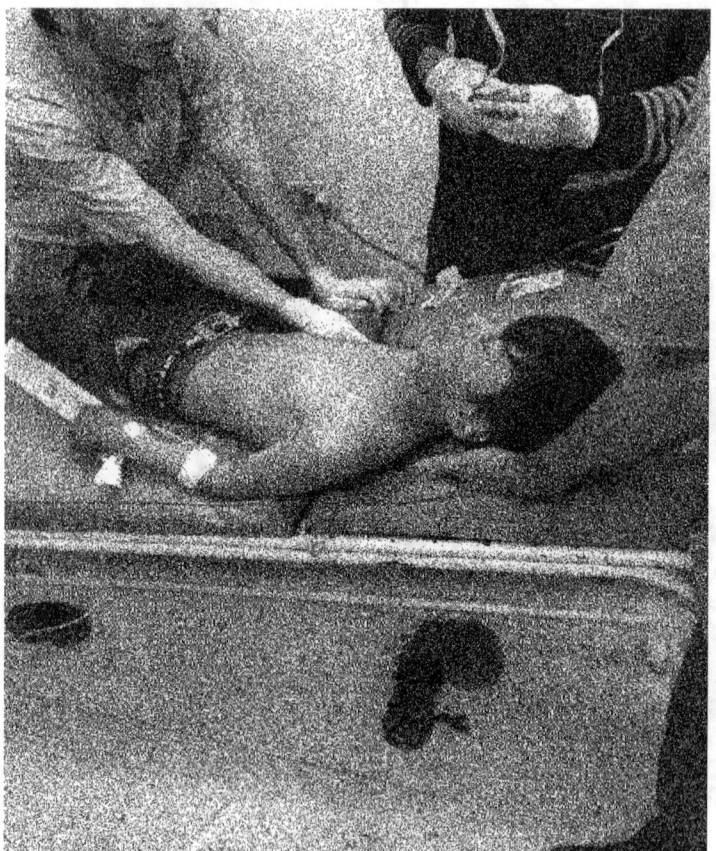

Local doctors in a SAMS hospital in Aleppo insert a chest tube into a child victim of barrel bombing.

International relief organizations such as the International Committee for the Red Cross and the Red Crescent, OXFAM, Save the Children, and the UN, are usually the main providers of medical and humanitarian relief in most disasters zones. However, such organizations are noticeably absent from relief efforts inside Syria. These large, established agencies are hampered by the real or perceived challenges of operating in a complex conflict zone. Security

[19]Sengupta, Somini. "U.N. Seeking More Ways to Distribute Aid in Syria." *The New York Times*. The New York Times, 17 May 2014. Web. 18 May 2014. <http://www.nytimes.com/2014/05/18/world/middleeast/un-seeking-more-ways-to-distribute-aid-in-syria.html?_r=0>.

concerns, roadblocks, bureaucratic hurdles, inflexible policies, inaccurate needs assessments, and an absence of a UNSC resolution for cross-border relief, have resulted in the absence of these organizations where they are needed most. Tens of thousands of Syrian civilians have died from preventable causes, not because of direct injuries from violence, but due to malnutrition, starvation, and a shortage of medications. Only recently, following UNSC Resolution 2139, has UNOCHA stepped up efforts to coordinate relief with Diaspora and international NGOs.

Volunteer doctors crossing the border as part of a SAMS medical missions to Syria

With a few exceptions, Syria's neighbors have provided basic shelter and health services to those in need and have absorbed millions of Syrian refugees forced to flee their country. In Turkey, the government has spent more than 2.5 billion dollars on Syrian refugees, providing free shelter, food, medical care, education and other services to more than 740,000 Syrian refugees living in the country.[20] In Jordan, the government has provided shelter and shared its scarce resources with the 600,000 Syrians taking refuge in the country. Syrian children enroll in Jordanian schools and Syrian patients receive medical care in state hospitals. In Lebanon, local NGOs and civic organizations mobilized to provide much-needed services to Syrian refugees in spite of the delicate demographic and political balance in their small country. Host to over a million Syrian refugees, Lebanon's capacity for humanitarian aid is overstretched, and more help is needed to address refugees' basic needs of shelter, medical care, psychosocial support, and education. Iraq became a refuge for a large population of Kurdish Syrian refugees fleeing from Northeastern Syrian Governorates.

---

[20] "Turkey RRP6: Monthly Update - March" UNHCR, March 2014. Web. May 18, 2014.
<http://data.unhcr.org/syrianrefugees/download.php?id=5429>

In spite of their limited capacity, local NGOs, especially the Syrian Red Crescent, stepped up their efforts to provide lifesaving humanitarian and medical relief to local Syrian populations and the internally displaced. Syrian Diaspora NGOs, including SAMS, are providing services in most areas inside Syria and coordinating effectively with local NGOs and civic councils to build an infrastructure for medical and humanitarian assistance. They have successfully addressed many obstacles stemming from the lack of capacity, access, security, and the lack of support from more established international NGOs and the UN.

So far the United States has provided more than 1.7 billion dollars in humanitarian assistance, making it the largest donor of humanitarian aid to Syria. Most of the humanitarian aid goes through UN agencies, although an increasing percentage is being awarded to international and regional NGOs. Local NGOs should receive an increased percentage of the funding because they have the expertise necessary to assess the needs on the ground. These NGOs have access to besieged areas, while the UN does not. Syrian organizations like SAMS engage directly with physicians on the ground and can utilize aid more effectively by establishing medical points and field hospitals as soon as violence intensifies in a given area. This flexibility is important when responding to chemical attacks because it minimizes casualties.

A mere 20 years ago, the world witnessed a horrific humanitarian tragedy in Rwanda. Our capabilities to respond to such crises have significantly increased in the years that followed. It is the responsibility of the United States and its citizens to advocate for greater humanitarian access, so that such tragedies are never repeated. During my trip to Aleppo last month, I witnessed the impact of indiscriminate barrel bombings attacks on Syria's largest city. I visited Aleppo numerous times between October and November. Since the barrel bombing campaigns began in November, the once vibrant center of Syria is now a ghost town. Because of the constant fear, people left their homes, leaving entire neighborhoods deserted.

When people hear about barrel bombs in the news, it is difficult for them to visualize the amount of damage these improvised explosives can inflict. Barrel bombs consist of an oil drum loaded with explosives and shards of metal. The Syrian government is using them in a systematic and indiscriminate manner. The purpose of these bombs is to harm civilians and to target medical facilities. Barrels bombs are indiscriminate weapons of war and their use is a violation of international law. More specifically, UN Security Council Resolution 2139 calls on all parties in the Syrian conflict to stop the use of indiscriminate weapons of war, including barrel bombs. Human Rights Watch reported that since late February, the city of Aleppo has been attacked by at least 85 barrel bombs, including direct attacks on hospitals in the city.[1]
SAMS's field hospitals in Aleppo and elsewhere in Syria have suffered barrel bomb attacks.

In Aleppo, a building adjacent to a SAMS field hospital was hit by an explosive barrel. Many patients and their family members were injured in the attack. Several floors of the hospital were damaged and the water and fuel systems were destroyed. During the evacuation of the hospital, a second barrel bomb was dropped on a nearby building.

Because of the systematic targeting of hospitals in Syria, local communities now view them as a threat, rather than a lifesaving service. For example, when a barrel bomb exploded near one of our field hospitals in Hama, the local population attributed the bombing to the existence of a hospital. Although the facility was not damaged, community members threatened members of the hospital staff and our facility was forced to close temporarily and then to relocate. It was not easy to find a new location as villages and towns actively resisted hosting the facility because civilians know that medical facilities are specifically targeted.

As a result, our field hospitals are now forced to work underground or as mobile clinics. Our hospital staff has adapted with the help of the local population. Community members notify SAMS doctors when barrel bomb attacks are imminent, so the doctors can safely take cover. However, such measure never suffice. Patients and doctors in underground operating rooms can not hear approaching helicopters, and can not escape in time.

SAMS, our partners, and other local and international NGOs, cannot continue to treat Syrians while our facilities and staff members are targeted by barrel bombs. SAMS calls on the president and allied world leaders to ensure that all parties in the Syrian conflict comply with UN Security Council Resolution 2139, which demands the end of "indiscriminate employment of weapons in populated areas including shelling and aerial bombardment, such as the use of barrel bombs." I urge the president to partner with the international community to end barrel bomb attacks by any means necessary, and ensure that they can not be used in Syria to actively obstruct the provision of humanitarian aid and medical care.

Barrel bombs are not the only weapons used to destroy medical facilities inside Syria. Our hospitals and medical personnel endure shelling from MiG airplanes on a daily basis. This is no accident. Medical facilities and medical personnel are actively targeted. Efforts by international organizations like Physicians for Human Rights and the International Committee for the Red Cross to monitor attacks on medical facilities corroborate this statement. In the Syrian conflict, targeting medical facilities and medical personnel is a tactic of war. In most conflict situations, the International Committee for the Red Cross recommends that its logo be displayed on all ambulances and facilities to protect them from attacks. In Syria, however, the ICRC recommends the opposite, because Red Crescent logos ensure that medical facilities and staff are targeted. The targeting of medical facilities and personnel is a direct of violation of the Geneva Convention.

Furthermore, the targeting of medical facilities and personnel directly impacts the efficacy of US humanitarian aid. The US government donates the most humanitarian aid to Syria, be it through the United Nations or direct funding to international relief organizations. This funding is used to provide medical facilities in Syria with medicine, medical supplies, and equipment. US government funding has made it possible to deliver equipment such as X-ray machines, ICU-ventilators, dialysis machines, operating tables, monitors, and blood bank equipment to facilities across Syria. Every time a facility is targeted, expensive equipment is damaged or destroyed, valuable medications are lost, and simple but lifesaving supplies like gauze and bandages are ruined. It is in the best interests of the US government to ensure that its funds are not wasted on the equipment and supplies lost to barrel bomb attacks. When our facilities are attacked, medical staff first search through the rubble for survivors, and then try to salvage supplies, medication, and equipment. Without these, they can not treat the victims of the barrel bombs or the shelling. Ending barrel bomb attacks would ensure that US government aid is effectively utilized in meeting the US objective of saving Syrian lives and mitigating the human cost of this crisis.

The use of chemical weapons has also contributed to the destruction of cities and villages on a massive scale. There are documented cases of chemical weapons use by the Syrian regime in more than 10 attacks. In three of these attacks 5 civilians were killed and 1000 admitted with respiratory and neurologic symptoms most likely due to the exposure to chlorine gas. The report of three chlorine attacks in Hama and Idlib provinces in April demonstrate the increased use of chlorine gas in this crisis. The healthcare system in Syria is on the verge of collapse. With the help of the few NGOs that remain in Syria, SAMS's field hospitals treat victims of chemical weapons attacks in hard-to-access areas. When chemical attacks devastated Rural Damascus last August and claimed over one thousand innocent Syrian lives, SAMS volunteers were at the scene saving lives. Before the attacks, SAMS trained area doctors in trauma care and provided them with protective gear, antidotes, and oxygen generators. One of our volunteers gathered samples from the chemical weapon attack victims as evidence of these heinous crimes.

In late April, SAMS received 16 cases of victims of a chlorine gas attack in the suburbs of Idlib. SAMS physicians treated all 16 victims with no reported deaths. SAMS staff also treated victims of chemical weapons attacks in Hama, where barrel bombs containing chlorine gas were dropped. Our hospitals in southern Syria have also received cases of poisonous gas attacks. On March 27, one of our field hospitals admitted 25 cases. Victims had symptoms of suffocation from being exposed to fumes with a strange odor and a white color. SAMS and its doctors saved 21 of these victims.

We believe that chemical weapon attacks will continue to kill and severely harm countless innocent Syrian civilians unless strong measures are taken immediately. The funding that is currently available to medical aid organizations will be insufficient to sustain the treatment of victims of chemical attacks, barrel bombings, and indiscriminate shelling. We strongly urge the House of Representatives to approve the $1.1 in assistance requested for FY15 budget, if not more.

The systematic and continuous targeting of medical facilities and medical personnel has led to the disintegration of the health care system in Syria. Local production of medicines has fallen by 90%. According to SAMS internal assessments and the WHO, medications, including anesthetics, analgesics, antibiotics, intravenous fluids, and medicines for the treatment of chronic diseases, are in short supply.[21] There has been a 75% decrease in pharmaceutical

---

[21] "Health: Syrian Arab Republic 2013." World Health Organization, 6 June 2013. Web. 19 May 2014. <http://www.who.int/hac/syria_dashboard_6june2013_final_small_.pdf>

production since 2010, and 25 pharmaceutical plants have been destroyed.[22] Not only has pharmaceutical production been damaged, the health infrastructure as a whole has been severely affected. In Dar'a, 44% of facilities are out of service and 33% are partially damaged, where 28% of the population is in need of aid.[23] In Rural Damascus, 50% of public hospitals are not in service and 30% are partially damaged. 44% of the population of Rural Damascus is in need of aid where only 20% of public hospital facilities are functioning and have no damage.[24] WHO reports that Al-Qutaifa and Jeroud public hospitals are the only two public hospitals serving Rural Damascus where approximately 1,255,833 Syrians are estimated to be in need of humanitarian aid. Tens of thousands of Syrian doctors, nurses, and hospital staff have fled the country to escape the violence. Medical professionals in Syria face heightened risks given the repeated targeting of healthcare facilities and staff. According to the UNFPA, an estimated 30,000 Syrian physicians have fled the country.[25] In some communities in Syria, the shortage of doctors is especially dire. For example, Eastern Ghota had 1,000 doctors before the war and as of December 2013, only an estimated 30 remain.[26]

As a result of the conflict, many Syrians die every day from otherwise manageable chronic conditions. The disruption of health care effects patients who rely on stable access the most, like patients undergoing dialysis treatments or undergoing treatment for cancer. According to field assessment conducted by SAMS 200,099 Syrians have succumbed to chronic conditions like diabetes, hypertension, and cancer. Before the crisis, Syria boasted a robust healthcare system that ensured patients treatment for chronic conditions. This is no longer the possible and chronic diseases, like kidney diseases, are affecting patients across Northern Syria. Many patients are dying from lack of dialysis treatments. There are consistently fewer and fewer sessions available for these patients. Equipment is outdated and malfunctioning along with a diminishing number of specialists and technicians. The few remaining facilities do not have the proper resources and supplies to adequately carry out operations. According to reports from SAMS partners on the ground and from SAMS physicians that went on medical missions to Syria, in Al Raqqah, 24 dialysis patients died this past November, and 37 patients died between December 18 and January 29 because of the lack of adequate health care. In Al Raqqah for instance, only 11 machines are still operating and they are supposed to serve the large amount of patients that comes to facility daily to seek treatment.

SAMS's mobile clinics around Syria are have reported warning signs of potential future epidemics. The three SAMS mobile clinics treated 4,427 total cases between February and April 2014. The caseload received by these clinics is important to track the spread of diseases and

---

[22] "Impact on Public Health Infrastructure & Workforce, as of 1st of October 2013." World Health Organization, October 2013. Web. 19 May 2014.

<http://www.who.int/hac/crises/syr/syria_impact_infrastucture_health_workforce_1october2013.pdf?ua=1>

[23] Ibid.

[24] Ibid.

[25] Rep. UNFPA, June 2013. Web. 19 May 2014.

<http://www.who.int/hac/crises/syr/syria_impact_infrastucture_health_workforce_1october2013.pdf?ua=1>.

[26] "Syria's Medical Community Under Assault." - Syria's Medical Community Under Assault. Physicians for Human Rights, May 2014. Web. 19 May 2014. <https://s3.amazonaws.com/PHR_other/Syria%27s-Medical-Community-Under-Assault-May-2014.pdf>.

epidemics. For instance, through caseload, SAMS has been able to document 83 cases of scabies, 34 cases of measles and 22 cases of Leishmaniasis in the past three months alone.

By continuing as the largest contributor of humanitarian aid to civilians in Syria, the United States can help curb the spread of epidemics and can continue to save lives. By supporting relief organizations and local NGOs, the US government can ensure that aid reaches the largest amount of beneficiaries, and that it reaches critical areas and the areas under siege. SAMS is pleased that the UN has finally started coordination efforts and SAMS supports this initiative and is an active member of the coordination meetings and working groups. However, SAMS urges the administration to channel most of the aid directly through relief organizations in order to maximize the effectiveness of this support.

We respectfully ask that the administration increase aid to Syria given the increased human suffering caused by barrel bombs and chlorine attacks and that this funding continue to go through relief organizations directly. We also ask that more funding be allocated towards capacity building for local NGOs. It is important that we begin to train local NGOs so that they will be ready to rebuild Syria soon after the crisis ends.

The future of Syria depends on the action we take today. Not acting to prevent further attacks on innocent civilians, medical facilities, and humanitarian actors today will only exacerbate the future medical and social problems that will prevail in a post-conflict Syria. It is the duty of the US government and all American citizens to enforce the Geneva conventions and to protect the lives of Syrian civilians. We call upon the US government to first and foremost put an end to barrel bombs and chemical attacks using any means at its disposal.

Ms. Ros-Lehtinen. Ms. Romero.

STATEMENT OF MS. BERNICE ROMERO, SENIOR DIRECTOR OF POLICY AND ADVOCACY, SAVE THE CHILDREN

Ms. Romero. First of all, I just want to thank Chairwoman Ros-Lehtinen and Ranking Member Deutch and the members of the subcommittee for the hearing.

Ms. Ros-Lehtinen. Can you put the microphone a little bit closer. Thanks.

Ms. Romero. Does that work?

The Syrian conflict has taken a devastating toll on Syria's children; 4.3 million need assistance and more than 10,000 young lives have been lost. Save the Children has worked in the Middle East for decades, providing assistance to over 1.6 million people, including 1.2 million children.

My remarks draw on our experience addressing the needs of children affected by the Syrian crisis. I will focus on two issues. One, education, particularly in Lebanon, and, two, child protection, especially child labor in Jordan. I will also mention two crucial issues, humanitarian funding and improved humanitarian access.

Continued education in crises is critical. It can give children a sense of stability, provide protection, and tell children they have a future, but many Syrian children face huge barriers to continuing their education. In fact, 3 million children have now dropped out of school in Syria, and 68 percent of refugee children are not in school. There are many challenges in host countries—overcrowding, high dropout rates, and lessons in languages the children don't even understand. For many, just getting to school is too expensive or they don't want to go because they are afraid of being bullied. Educational challenges are especially acute in Lebanon, which has received a staggering number of refugees, somewhere between 1 and 1.5 million. Lebanon would have to more than double its current education infrastructure to meet the needs of Syrian children. Less than 20 percent are currently enrolled, and dropout rates reach up to 40 percent. Children are being sent instead out to work in fields for $2 a day or others as young as 3 can be seen begging in the streets. Skills training for youth is limited, leaving them with unstructured days, few job opportunities, and little hope.

We need to start having hard conversations on how to tackle the problems that are stopping Syrian children from learning, not just in Lebanon but throughout the region. That needs to happen now. Already most have lost up to 3 years of school. A long-term plan that prioritizes, protects, and enables refugee education in host countries needs to be developed urgently. The international community needs to fund it and help host countries shoulder the burden. We urge the U.S. to work with others and support host country efforts to expand educational infrastructure, vocational training programs, and nonformal learning centers. Host governments can't do it alone, and Syria's future depends on the skills and knowledge these children gain today.

Inside Syria children are being killed and injured and witnessing or experiencing atrocities. Three out of four children have now lost a loved one to the conflict and reports of early marriage, sexual abuse, and domestic violence are rising.

According to UNICEF, 1 in 10 children across the region is now engaged in some form of child labor. The problem may be greatest in Jordan where children are often working in hazardous industries. Eighty percent of girls working in Jordan are in domestic labor or agriculture, both known for high levels of sexual exploitation. The main reason children are working is to support their families. Syrians can't officially work in Jordan and a number of studies show a direct link between the lack of livelihoods, opportunities, and the high levels of child labor. Namely, it is easier for a child to find work, and the ramifications for a child caught working illegally are less severe. As a result, Syrian refugees rely heavily on child labor to supplement family income. Of the households that reported paid labor in the past month, 47 percent reported that some or all of this income was from children. The Government of Jordan has been generous, but the problem requires U.S. and other donor support to ensure policy reforms that protect children in informal labor and programs that provide job training and opportunities and provide financial support.

Children inside Syria face additional protection challenges to deal with the direct violence of war. The U.S. should use its influence to ensure parties to the conflict agree not to target or allow military use of schools or health facilities and agree not to use explosive weapons in populated areas, the primary reported cause of children's deaths.

Despite the challenges, aid is making a difference. We urge Congress to protect U.S. humanitarian accounts against cuts. We also need improved access to people living inside Syria, U.N. Resolution 2139, to allow humanitarian access was a political breakthrough, but nearly 3 months after its adoption, only a trickle of the aid is making it through. Every day that goes by without access is another fatal day for children. Congress should send a clear message about the importance of humanitarian access, pushing for the resolution's full implementation and encouraging U.N. agencies to fund cross-border aid and increase their important coordination role.

There is a risk that Syria will become just another conflict that we all view as hopeless and therefore ignore, but the children of Syria deserve better. We look to you for the support needed to reduce current suffering and improve the future outlook for Syria's children. Thank you.

Ms. ROS-LEHTINEN. Thank you so much, Ms. Romero.

[The prepared statement of Ms. Romero follows:]

 **Save the Children.**

Testimony on "The Humanitarian Crisis in Syria: Views from the Ground"
for the House Foreign Affairs Subcommittee on the Middle East and North Africa

Wednesday, May 21, 2014

Bernice G Romero, Senior Director, Public Policy and Advocacy, Humanitarian Response

I want to thank Chairwoman Ros-Lehtinen and Ranking Member Deutch for organizing today's hearing on the humanitarian crisis in Syria.

Three years of conflict in Syria have taken a devastating toll on Syria's children. The scale, brutality and duration of the conflict have created levels of need almost impossible to imagine. 4.3 million children in Syria are in desperate need of assistance and more than 10,000 young lives have been lost. The plight of these children may be the most serious humanitarian crisis of our generation with consequences for many generations to come.

Save the Children has worked in the Middle East for decades to advance our mission as a nonprofit, child-focused agency working to inspire breakthroughs in the way the world treats children and to achieve immediate and lasting change in their lives. Today we are working with communities, host governments and UN agencies to ensure that all vulnerable groups affected by the Syrian conflict get the assistance and protection they need. To date, we have provided lifesaving assistance such as shelter, food and protection to over 1.6 million people in Lebanon, Jordan, Iraq, Egypt and Syria –nearly 1.2 million of whom are children.

My recommendations to Congress and the Administration draw upon Save the Children's experience working to address the needs of children and families affected by the Syrian crisis. Today I will focus on four issues. First, I will discuss the value of investing in education to ensure that refugee children have access to safe learning environments and gain the knowledge and skills necessary for Syria's future. I will examine several barriers to education that refugee children are facing, particularly in Lebanon. Second, I will discuss the importance of supporting child protection activities to help refugee children cope with trauma they have experienced as a result of the crisis. I will focus particularly on the child protection concern of child labor in Jordan. Third, I will discuss the importance of robustly funding humanitarian accounts to ensure that lifesaving assistance is available for families and children affected by the crisis. Finally, I will discuss steps Congress can take to improve humanitarian access to ensure that lifesaving aid can reach children and families living in besieged and hard-to-reach areas.

Ultimately, ending the conflict in Syria is the only way to end the suffering of Syria's children. Until a political solution is found, however, we can take steps to build a better future for Syria's children. Save the Children, together with UNICEF, UNCHR, World Vision, Mercy Corps, CARE and other partners have launched the "No Lost Generation" campaign to help address the enormous needs of children in the region. With this campaign, we are calling on the international community to provide $1 billion to help rescue a generation of Syrian children from lives of despair and broken futures. We seek to accelerate donor and public support for programs that help Syrian children gain access to quality education, protect them from violence and abuse, and provide counseling and psychological support. Without more investment in education and child protection, we risk losing an entire generation – the very people who will eventually be called on to help Syria rebuild and recover.

Education

Funding for education programming for children is critical. Education is a key stabilizing force in the lives of children affected by conflict. It can give children hope, provide physical and psychosocial protection, and send children the message that the world has not given up on their future. Despite these important benefits, many children are not in school and face huge barriers to continuing their education. Consider the following:

- Three million children have now dropped out of school in Syria
- One in five schools has been damaged or destroyed
- 22% of teaching staff and 18% of school counselors have left the country
- 68% of refugee children are not in school – in Lebanon this is as high as 80%

We know from our work in Lebanon, Jordan, Iraq and Egypt that countries across the region face many of the same educational policy problems, challenges, and gaps. Schools are overcrowded and Syrian children are being turned away. Many are dropping out because they do not understand the lessons or the language in which they are being taught. Others have fallen far behind and there are few opportunities for them to catch up or alternative ways for them to learn. Most don't know if their learning will be recognized later by school systems or employers. A large number have to abandon education and go to work in order to support their families.

Educational challenges are especially acute in Lebanon. Lebanon has received a staggering number of refugees—somewhere between I and 1.5 million or roughly a quarter to one third of its population. This is placing a huge amount of pressure on a country that is already struggling with political instability. Lebanon now has the highest concentration in the world of refugees as a percentage of population, with about one Syrian for every three Lebanese. In order to provide an adequate education for Syrian refugee children, Lebanon would have to more than double its education infrastructure and school capacity.

Less than 20% of Syrian children are currently enrolled in full time formal education in Lebanon's public school system. For many of the reasons outlined above—including language challenges, economic need, and sometimes bullying by other students—drop-out rates are extremely high among those few enrolled in full time formal education, reaching up to 40%. Children out of school are often being sent out to work in fields for as little as two dollars a day. Others, as young as three years old, can be seen begging on the streets of towns and cities. Skills-training is also limited, leaving disenfranchised youth with unstructured days, few employment opportunities, and little hope for their future. For the countless thousands of youth who have lost friends and family to Syria's brutal war and who find themselves without opportunity, radicalization, criminalization and militarization may seem to be some of the few options available.

The international community must do much more to provide the government of Lebanon with the necessary support to ensure that refugee children can access education. This includes providing support for community based education efforts where INGOs and UN agencies can work together to provide high quality, formal education to Syrian children in non-formal surroundings and supporting the government of Lebanon in the rehabilitation and extension of existing school facilities and the training of teachers. At present the Lebanese government is also providing a "second shift" system which allows Syrian students to attend school and avail of a truncated curriculum for around three hours a day when the normal public school day ends. This should be complemented by community based efforts. Using existing structures or setting up easy to assemble structures where required, teachers can be trained, accredited and deployed; the Lebanese curriculum can be adapted; and accreditation can be provided to students, enabling them to progress to higher level education and training. This approach is one that can be deployed speedily and reach large numbers of children.

We need to start having some hard conversations on how we are going to tackle some of the big, persistent problems that are stopping Syrian children from learning and developing not just in Lebanon but throughout the region. The window to take effective action is closing fast. Most Syrian refugee children have lost up to three years of school already and a clear plan is needed to ensure yet another year is not lost so that Syrian children can develop to their full potential. Syria's future depends on it. A comprehensive, long-term plan on how to prioritize, protect and enable refugee education in the countries surrounding Syria needs to be developed by key stakeholders, including national governments, so that education can be delivered in a comprehensive, efficient and coordinated way. The international community needs to fund it and help national governments shoulder the burden. To this end, we urge the US to work with other donors to:

- Support programs throughout the region that provide Syrian refugee children with access to education, whether at school or through learning programs. Only one third of refugee children currently have such access;

- Support host country efforts to expand educational infrastructure to accommodate refugee children including hiring more teachers and providing materials and resources for additional teaching shifts

- Invest in programming that helps both refugee and local children from the host country to learn together

- Support vocational training programs and non-formal learning centers

Child Protection

Funding for child protection programming is critical because the crisis has put already vulnerable children at risk of harm. Every day in Syria's brutal war, children are being killed or injured. They are also witnessing and experiencing atrocities that no one—much less a child—should ever see. The resulting trauma is profound. Consider the following:

- Three out of four children have now lost a loved one to the conflict and the atrocities they have witnessed have left them with deep emotional scars;

- Early marriage is now affecting one in five girls; this time last year it was affecting one in eight girls;

- Sexual abuse and domestic violence is increasingly being reported;

- Children are at risk of recruitment by armed groups, both as fighters or as support to military groups as runners, cooks and cleaners;

- About 8,000 children across the region are estimated to have been separated from their families and are living unaccompanied;

- UNICEF estimates one in ten children across the region is now engaged in some form of child labor. A recent Save the Children assessment in one governorate puts this number as high as 91% in some border towns.

While child labor is an issue of concern across the region, Save the Children's research shows this may be much higher in Jordan. Children are working in the worst forms of labor, often in industries that are hazardous for their health and wellbeing. 80% of girls working in Jordan are in domestic labor or agriculture—industries known for high levels of sexual exploitation. While child labor in Jordan has been shown to affect boys more than girls, Save the Children assessments highlight a particular category of girls in exploitative work, which is not normally considered child labor—"homebound girls". These are girls who have been withdrawn from school, confined to the family home and engaged in household chores on a full time basis.

The main reason children are working is to support their families. There is a substantial risk that, without alternatives, child labor will increase for both poorer Jordanian and Syrian children. For Jordanian children, the refugee crisis has put pressure on resources for the poorest families in Jordan, particularly in the northern border area, which is one of the most impoverished regions in the country.

Currently, Syrians cannot officially work in Jordan, and a number of studies show a direct link between the lack of livelihood opportunities and the high levels of child labor—namely it's easier for a child to find work than it is for adults to find work and the ramifications of a child being caught working illegally are less severe. In a recent UN survey, 30% of respondents reported having at least one family member find paid employment during the past month in Jordan. As a result, Syrian refugees rely heavily on child labor to supplement family income. Almost 15% of all households surveyed cited child labor as their primary source of income.[1] Of the households that reported paid labor in the past month 47% reported that some or all of this income was from children.

The government of Jordan has been generous in its reception of Syrian refugees. According to UNHCR, the total number of registered Syrian refugees in Jordan is 591,922, with over half of these arriving in 2013. The government of Jordan estimates there are now over 600,000 Syrians in the country, of which over half are children. The scale of the problem necessitates US and other governments' support to ensure:

- Policy reforms that protect children in informal labor and look at what job training and opportunities can be provided where refugees can contribute to economic growth and development

- Strengthened educational services and policies to keep children safe in school

- Programs to promote livelihoods and provide financial support through programs like cash-for-work

---

[1] UN Women Report, *"Gender-based violence and child protection among Syrian refugees in Jordan, with a focus on early marriage", p20*

Children inside Syria face additional protection challenges to do with the direct violence they are witnessing and experiencing. The US and other governments should use diplomatic influence to ensure that all parties to the conflict:

- Agree not to target or allow military use of schools or health facilities. Since the conflict started, nearly 1 in 5 schools inside Syria have been damaged, destroyed, used by the military, or turned into shelters. Putting schools out of use in this way not only makes schools unusable or unsafe, but also can make children fearful of going back to school when the conflict ends. Health facilities have also been targeted, putting children at risk.

- Agree not to use explosive weapons in populated areas. To date, the primary cause of death of children in the Syrian conflict has been explosive weapons, killing over 70% of children whose cause of death was recorded. We must put a stop to the killing and maiming of children. All parties to conflict should refrain from the use of explosive weapons with wide area effects in populated areas to ensure that civilians – in particular children – are protected against death, injury and psychological harm.

Humanitarian Funding

As difficult as daily life is for millions in the region, the situation is not hopeless, and international assistance is making a difference. In December, the UN launched an unprecedented appeal for $6.5 billion in 2014 to assist the millions of people affected by Syria's conflict—the largest humanitarian appeal ever. Many donor governments, including the United States, have been generous in providing financial support to help Syrian refugees. However, more funding is required to meet the mounting needs as the crisis continues into its fourth year.

Despite the great humanitarian need, President Obama's proposed FY2015 budget slashed overall humanitarian assistance by 25% below the funding level Congress provided for humanitarian accounts in the FY2014 omnibus spending bill passed in January. Specific cuts proposed by the Administration include:

- 33% cut to the Migration and Refugee account that supports refugee response

- 28% cut to the International Disaster Assistance account that supports internally displaced people

- 4.5% cut to the Food for Peace program, which feeds tens of millions of people around the world. This cut represents reducing food assistance to more than 1.5 million people.

Cutting the humanitarian accounts by 25% means that funding the Syrian response would have to be done at the expense of reducing assistance for life-threatening crises elsewhere, such as in the Central African Republic and South Sudan. As such, Save the Children is urging Congress to:

- Protect foreign assistance humanitarian accounts against the severe cuts proposed by the Administration in the budget to ensure that significant gains made in the FY14 appropriations bill are not lost.

- Use its influence to urge the Administration to pay special attention to host communities to help them deal with the refugee influx and its resulting strain on community resources. Across the region, almost 80% of Syria's refugees do not live in camps, but instead live with family or friends or in informal settlements. Supporting host communities is an important step to ensure that countries have the support they need to keep their borders open.

- Encourage the Administration to create a long-term strategy that integrates humanitarian response and development funding streams. Save the Children has advocated for the Administration to consider using resources from development accounts to fund programs that benefit communities that host refugees. We are also encouraging U.S. government agencies to do joint planning to ensure that humanitarian and development funding streams are used effectively to address the Syrian crisis.

Humanitarian Access

In addition to robust funding of the humanitarian response, humanitarian agencies need improved access to people living in besieged and hard-to-reach areas. Full humanitarian access would ensure medical care for injured children, food for starving families, clean water, shelter and some hope for the future.

On February 22, 2014, the UN Security Council unanimously passed UN Security Council Resolution 2139 to allow unfettered humanitarian access to all parts of Syria. The passage of this resolution was a political breakthrough that included strong stipulations demanding both cross-line and cross-border access. This resolution also demanded an end to sieges across the country, an end to the indiscriminate use of weapons in populated areas, and the demilitarization of medical facilities, schools and other civilian facilities.

However, nearly three months after the adoption of the UN Security Council Resolution, only a trickle of the aid desperately needed inside besieged and hard-to-reach areas is making it through. Around 3.5 million people are now estimated to be in need of assistance in such areas – an increase of one million since the beginning of this year.

Every day that goes by without the resolution fully implemented is another fatal day for more Syrian children and their families. Therefore, Congress should use its influence to send a clear message about the importance of humanitarian access. To this end, Save the Children suggests that Congress do the following:

- Use diplomatic pressure with governments that have influence over parties to the conflict to push for full implementation of UN Security Council Resolution 2139.

- Encourage UN agencies to increase funding for humanitarian NGOs providing assistance through cross-border channels. To this end, Congress should 1) urge the UN to immediately use pooled funding mechanisms such as the Emergency Relief Fund (ERF) to fund cross-border work carried out by humanitarian NGOs and 2) direct the Administration to provide resources through pooled funding mechanisms like the ERF for cross-border response.

- Encourage UN agencies to increase coordination and communication between Syria-based and cross border humanitarian providers. In order to ensure that aid coverage is effective and not duplicated or diverted, UN agencies should work in partnership with NGOs to develop communication lines between Damascus-based agencies and those providing assistance from neighboring countries.

- Advocate with neighboring government authorities to agree on a humanitarian fast track that can streamline and speed up the delivery of humanitarian aid, open additional border crossings, and diminish other administrative hurdles for INGOs delivering aid across borders.

- Request that the UN Secretary General include additional criteria in his monthly reports in order to collect information about the challenges NGOs face in cross-border operations.

- Encourage increased UN monitoring of access with information provided on when and where requests are being made and when these are accepted or denied.

*****

We thank the subcommittee for its leadership in addressing the needs of those affected by the Syrian crisis. We sincerely appreciate your attention to these important issues, and look to both the Administration and Congress to marshal the necessary support, including in upcoming appropriations legislation, to reduce the suffering and improve the outlook for the children and families of Syria. This is not only the right approach required by the scale of human suffering and America's long standing tradition of helping those in need, but also the smart approach for advancing U.S. interests in the region.

Ms. Ros-Lehtinen. Thank you, all of you, for being here to discuss the important work you do, the challenges that your organizations face, and what we need to do or change in order to ensure that our relief efforts are being maximized.

I want to extend a heartfelt thank you to each and every one of you and your organizations, who, in many instances, have caregivers and are risking their lives on a daily basis in order to get supplies to those in dire need. It is a dangerous job, and I am sure it is a rewarding job, but it is often a thankless job, at least by those who aren't directly impacted by your work on the ground in Syria. So thank you so much.

What more do you need from the U.S. and other donor countries? What is the most pressing issue that isn't being adequately addressed?

Ms. Koppel, we will start with you.

Ms. Koppel. Thank you, Madam Chairwoman. I would say, as many of my colleagues have already cited, to fund the—basically, for Fiscal Year 2015 funding, to restore the humanitarian assistance cuts that were made in the Fiscal Year 2015 request by the Obama administration, restore them to Fiscal Year 2014 levels, especially IDA, MRA, and Food for Peace. We would also urge you to use your influence with the administration to get the U.N. to fully implement 2139. But in doing so, with the U.N., if it were to move toward cross border, we need the U.N. to work on coordinating this cross border. We need to, as we heard some of the members mention, there are about 240,000 people who are estimated to be living in besieged communities. We have no idea how much, if any, aid is getting in. We need assessments to be made before we start delivering aid, and we need post distribution of reviews and monitoring to be made to ensure that the aid is reaching the most vulnerable. We need to be accountable for that. These are humanitarian principles that all of us must abide by. Thank you.

Ms. Ros-Lehtinen. Thank you. Anyone else? Ms. Solberg?

Ms. Solberg. Thank you. Thank you very much. I would just complement that by saying as well, I think, what we need is around the coordination with the United Nations, but really also support with developing a comprehensive strategy, so one that is actually addressing the humanitarian needs today but looking further into the future and supporting for livelihood opportunities as well, so it does fit in very closely with the need for the funding levels to be brought back to the levels that they were before.

Ms. Ros-Lehtinen. Thank you.

Doctor?

Dr. Sahloul. A few things. The first thing that the United Nations distribution of aid has been changed in the last year, and according to the reports, that 85 percent of food distribution and 75 percent of medical aid is distributed only through the regime-controlled areas. That means what is left to the 9.5 million people who live outside of the regime-controlled area is less than 15 percent of food supplies and 25 percent of medical aid, and these are the population who are in much need. So somehow we need to change this formula so we can support the organizations, the NGOs that are assisting the people who are in much need, not probably through the United Nations but through different ways. We have to change this, reverse this formula.

The other thing that I urge this committee and all House Members to support House Resolution 520 that calls the administration to expand humanitarian assistance and stop the attack on civilians. The attacks on civilians and hospitals and infrastructure is continuing unhampered, and it is causing more destruction of hospitals and clinics and bakeries and schools that we can build and that we can support. So unless we can stop the barrel bombing, unless we can stop the bombing of hospitals and schools, then whatever we do will not be able to sustain and support the population. The population in the City of Aleppo, which is the largest city in Syria, needs to breathe, needs to care about development. The civic society needs to work. And if you have 20 barrel bombs raining on you every day, no matter what we do, we cannot support them, so they are forced to be displaced. They are forced to be leaving to Turkey or to neighboring countries, and this is a huge problem. So somehow the administration has to stop that from happening.

Ms. ROS-LEHTINEN. Thank you.

Ms. Romero?

Ms. ROMERO. Yeah, I mean, I would support everything everyone has said already, particularly around the need for sustained funding and the need to support the access resolution, the implementation of that, and the emphasis on cross-border aid, adding to that the need for more funding specifically for cross-border aid, more flexible funding models than what we have at present, but also the use of the U.S.'s good offices in terms of diplomatic pressure on other donors, particularly nontraditional donors. It is outrageous that we are fronting like almost 25 percent of all of this, and also more support to host countries in a more long-term sustainable way, particularly around child-specific issues. I mean, they do represent 50 percent of those that are being affected, and they are the future of Syria and of stability in the region, so a bigger investment in children.

Ms. ROS-LEHTINEN. Thank you very much.

Thank you to all of you. I think we have time for Mr. Deutch's questions before we will be interrupted by a vote. Mr. Deutch is recognized.

Mr. DEUTCH. Thank you, Madam Chairman.

First, thanks to all of you for testimony that was as powerful as the work that you are doing on the ground.

I learned a new term a couple weeks back. Perhaps you have heard of it. Psychic numbing. Are you familiar with the term? I wasn't. And it was used in response to a question that I asked about how we make this awful tragedy, the worst humanitarian crisis that most of us have seen, how we make this relevant to so many people who don't think about it. So that, as, Ms. Romero, you said, this doesn't just become another conflict that we all view as hopeless.

Ms. ROMERO. Yeah.

Mr. DEUTCH. So how do we do it? This is a really important discussion about funding and putting pressure on others to step up. But how do we—all of you work with groups and are there on the ground every day.

Dr. Sahloul, let me start with you. You discussed what happens when chlorine is used. I just hope that you can spend a minute telling us what a barrel bomb is. What is it? Who is it dropped on, and what does it do?

Dr. SAHLOUL. I have seen it, and actually, one of the most common scenes and bizarre scenes that you face in the City of Aleppo that when you are walking, and I walk in the street in some of the neighborhoods, you see people pointing to the sky and then you see this small dot which is a helicopter, and then suddenly this small dot will throw another dot, and it takes about 20 to 30 seconds for that dot to come and explode, and this is a barrel bomb. Barrel bomb is a barrel that is stuffed with TNT. We are not talking about a small amount of TNT; 200 to 500 kilograms of TNT, that can cause the destruction of one whole block and a lot of killing. I have seen the consequences of that in the hospital when you bring patients who are injured and amputated and killed because of this, and lately, these barrel bombs have been stuffed not only with TNT and shrapnel and petrol but also with chlorine gas, according to the report. I have talked with physicians who are treating these patients who are exposed to chlorine gas. It is a very choking gas, and it can cause death, and it is a chemical agent. It is a prohibited agent. It is one of the agents that is prohibited by the conventional chemical weapons convention that Syria has signed on it, and it has been used frequently in the last few months, and we are not doing anything.

Mr. DEUTCH. Dr. Sahloul, what happens when it is dropped on a school?

Dr. SAHLOUL. I have seen children, pictures, of course, and I have talked with physicians who have treated these children, people start to choke. Then they will start to have coughing, and sometimes you will have irritation of the skin and the eyes. Then they stop breathing, and many of them are transported to the emergency room and the hospital that are not equipped to treat chemical weapon attacks and chemical weapon agents. We are talking about a country in crisis, where the healthcare system has been already destroyed, and then you have chemical agents dropped on them on a daily basis, and the world is not paying attention. I mean, I agree with you that why is it that the world is not paying attention to this? I mean, I know that the crisis has been going on for 3 years, but we have children who are dying every day, we have people who are affected every day, more than the people who are affected by Boko Haram. I mean, we are not seeing policymakers speaking about the issue in Syria. I think we have to have leadership in this country that cares about the Syrian fight, which I believe that they care, but also make sure that this is in the public sphere. When the President of the United States or the Secretary Kerry talk about what is happening in Syria to the American public, I think they will care. You will see more support to humanitarian assistance, you have churches and synagogues that will donate, as they have donated to Haiti, for example. They are not doing that for Syria because Syria is away from the public eye.

Mr. DEUTCH. Okay. Let me just ask, and anyone jump in, but there are—you know, what we hear all the time, and this is my concern, Ms. Romero, when you talk about the way the crisis in

Syria is viewed, what we hear all the time is, well, it is really hard for us to know what to do, because there are so many different people fighting one another and it is hard to tell who we can support, who are the worst parties, and so, therefore, we will try to help on a humanitarian level.

What can any of you tell us to make this more urgent, to make all of us understand what you devote so much of your time to this crisis? Ms. Koppel.

Ms. KOPPEL. Ranking Member Deutch, we struggle with this as well. Many of us in—when there is some kind of a natural disaster, like the cyclone in the Philippines or the earthquake in Haiti, are surprised by the extent of the generosity of the American public. This is a protracted crisis. We are in our fourth year, and people have become numb. I think it isn't, as the good doctor mentioned, in the public sphere.

You are going home for the Memorial Day recess. I would urge you to talk to your constituents about the fact that if this were the United States, that would be the equivalent, if you are looking at Lebanon with 25 percent of its population being refugees, of 79 million refugees in the United States. Who would be there to help us?

Mr. DEUTCH. Let me——

Ms. KOPPEL. And if I could just add one other thing. The solution—as much as we as humanitarian actors are responding to the need of the civilians, but the solution is a political one. We need to replace the special U.N. Envoy, Lakhdar Brahimi, as quickly as possible. He just resigned last week. There must be a political process and ultimately a political solution.

Mr. DEUTCH. I appreciate it, and—but just before I yield back, Madam Chairman, I appreciate trying to show us what the scale would be in this country. I would just suggest that for all of us who are going back to our districts, the school year is coming to an end, and the fact is that if any of us imagined any school in our district, any school in this country with kids on the playground looking up at a helicopter waiting for that dot to grow, knowing that it is a barrel full of TNT and shrapnel and perhaps chlorine that could strike at any moment and kill and maim and do grave damage, that would be enough, that would be enough to rally everyone in this country.

And I—again, I just have so much respect for what you all do and I really appreciate your being here. And I hope your being here and sharing the important work that you do and the horrible situation on the ground will help propel this debate forward so that we can plan——

Ms. ROS-LEHTINEN. Thank you very much, Mr. Deutch.

And we have zero time remaining for our votes, and so our subcommittee will hover, and we will vote and come back.

Mr. SCHNEIDER. Madam Chairman, if I can just have 2 seconds for one open question, not for an answer.

But as you said, Ms. Koppel, the only solution is a political solution; a military solution on either side would be a catastrophe. On the day that there is a political solution, if you could submit for the record, or just I invite for an ongoing conversation, what the scope, the scale and the duration of the ongoing work after that political solution to make sure that Lebanon, Jordan, Syria, the future of the region is one that has a positive future and not as a spiral downward. Thank you very much.

Ms. ROS-LEHTINEN. Thank you so much. So we will vote and come back with—we have members to ask questions. Thank you. Please excuse us.

[Recess.]

Ms. ROS-LEHTINEN. The subcommittee has reconvened. Thank you for your patience.

And we are honored to recognize Mr. Kinzinger, who is one of our many American heros on this panel. Thank you for your service.

Mr. KINZINGER. Oh, that is kind. Thank you very much.

Ms. ROS-LEHTINEN. You deserve it.

Mr. KINZINGER. Thank you.

And to the panel, as I said in my short opening statement, thank you very much for being here. This is a situation in Syria that is only going to get worse. You know, you look at what is happening, for instance, in Ukraine and Russia, and you know that if the worst happens there at some point, there will still be an end game to what is happening.

In Syria, you are only going to continue to see the problem grow and grow and spread and spread into places that we have always considered to be good allies, places that we have considered to be safe in the Middle East. Just look at Iraq. I believe it was an epic mistake to pull all the troops out of Iraq—that is for another hearing—but what you see in western Iraq right now is the increase in Al Qaeda and ISIS in part of, and partially because of, what is happening in Syria today. This is a very big deal.

Doctor, when you started talking about and documenting the use of chemical weapons—and hello, by the way, and thanks for being here—it really breaks my heart to see that this is still happening. America has always held that there would be a red line against chemical weapons use. In fact, we had two no-fly zones over Iraq for 10 years because of the use of chemical weapons, and I have been well documented in saying it was an epic mistake not to enforce the red line that the President put down, but let me ask you, sir, could you briefly talk just a little bit more about what you have seen and how often are these chemical weapons being used, even though it may be chlorine gas and not gas that we necessarily—well, why don't you just talk about what you have seen and a little more on that level.

Dr. SAHLOUL. Well, thank you very much for raising this point, because it is very important for the American public to know that the chemical weapon is still being used in Syria, and it is used against civilian population, and it is causing death and injuries among civilian population.

Since the beginning of this year, 2014, there were 16 incidents of chemical weapon use. The first few ones were around Damascus and the City of Harasta, and it did not attract that much attention because few people had symptoms or died. In the—since April 11th, where you had the largest attack in Kafr Zaita, which is a village north of Hama, Hama is the city—a major city in Syria, which I am sure that people are aware of, you know, it had a lot of population death at the time of the father of this President, Hafez al-

Assad, and about 200 people had symptoms, respiratory symptoms, and one or two died because of that. And this is the City of Kafr Zaita.

Since then, and the city—I mean, someone may ask, why is it this city? Because it is on a strategic supply road that connects Hama to Aleppo. Aleppo is a major city where there is a lot of fighting, and this village that is under the control of the opposition falls on that access road. And this village has been attacked five times so far. The last one was yesterday.

There is also another village in the city of—in the governance of Idlib that also had a major attack. We believe that it is chlorine gas, because of the symptoms. We believe that this is against the prohibition of chemical weapon convention, and we believe this is against the red lines that we put, and we believe that this is something that the world community and the United States administration has to pay attention to.

I made sure that when we received the medical report, to share it with the National Security Council, with the State Department and with Ambassador Power about 2 weeks ago. So every information that we get about chemical weapons use—and mostly it is medical and testimonial physicians and so forth—we share it with the administration.

Mr. KINZINGER. Well, thank you very much. And I just want to be very clear, too. As bad as chemical weapons are, we are also seeing, as you discussed, a terrible weapon being employed called barrel bombs, something that I had never heard of until this conflict, and now I realize how absolutely indiscriminate it is in who it kills and what it clears. I believe that the cost of Assad of using chemical weapons and using barrel bombs needs to exceed any benefit he gains from that, and that would be through, in my belief, military strikes.

Let me ask everybody on the panel, what impact would—I want to make one point, and then I will ask everybody on the panel. First off, I want to make it very clear that the Free Syrian Army has diverted resources against Assad to fight extremists, so there is a belief somehow in the American public that the opposition is all extreme. The Free Syrian Army has been very clear that they are fighting a two-front war at this point, both against the Assad regime and against the extremists in Syria.

Let me ask the question to all the panel, and then I am sure my time will be up. If the United States and the West were able to implement a no-fly zone over Syria, how would that impact the ability to deliver aid, both to populations outside of Syria and to populations within Syria?

And, Ms. Koppel, I guess we will start with you.

Ms. KOPPEL. Thank you, Congressman. I hope you will understand that as a humanitarian—representative of a humanitarian organization, we leave it to those experts in the military to provide advice on that, but what I can say is that in light of this very fluid theater and in light of the increasing danger in this theater inside Syria, it is incredibly important that we not politicize humanitarian assistance, that we keep these channels separate.

Organizations like ours operate on a community-based acceptance level. That means we don't drive in the MRAPs. We are not in armored cars. We don't have weapons. Our security, our insurance policy is the fact that the community knows that we are impartial and we are independent and we abide by the utmost humanitarian principles.

Mr. KINZINGER. Under——

Ms. KOPPEL. And so if humanitarian aid is given to those who have a political agenda, that puts a bull's eye on the backs of my colleagues who are risking their lives inside Syria, and, Congressman, it puts a bull's eye on the backs of the Syrian civilians who are receiving this assistance. So——

Mr. KINZINGER. So do barrel bombs. Those put a bull's eye on the back of Syrian civilians, too.

Madam Chair, can I ask for——

Ms. ROS-LEHTINEN. Of course, you can.

Mr. KINZINGER. Ms. Solberg, would you talk about—and, again, my question is just simply—you don't have to get into the politics of should we do a no-fly zone, but if we did a no-fly zone, how would that that help in terms of administering of aid?

Ms. SOLBERG. Thank you, Chairman. I would—sorry—congressman. I would say that I completely agree with what my colleague, Ms. Koppel, has said from that perspective.

What we know is that we are reaching maybe 10 percent of the people who need assistance inside Syria. The numbers continue to grow in neighboring countries. If we can have increased access from a very specific humanitarian perspective to get in and reach those people in need, that is what we are trying to do. And I would say from, again, following humanitarian principles, impartiality, reaching those in need, that is our objective.

Mr. KINZINGER. Right. Well understood.

Ms. Wanek.

Ms. WANEK. To echo my colleagues as well, as a humanitarian organization, we very much don't—don't comment on nor have——

Mr. KINZINGER. I understand all that; you guys can't advocate, but would it happy in terms—is your access limited because people are being bombed and killed?

Ms. WANEK. I think we had need to do everything we can to provide humanitarian assistance in an impartial manner to those that are affected that are the most vulnerable.

Mr. KINZINGER. And, Doctor, what about you?

Dr. SAHLOUL. I can tell you that in the last 6 months, we had four of our hospitals that were supported by tax money bombed by barrel bombs. One of them actually was bombed by a guided missile. So, definitely, if we have a way to reduce the impact of these weapons of mass destruction, I mean, I am talking about barrel bombs, 500 kilograms of TNT, then that will make it easier for us to perform our operation, and also it would make it easier for refugees and displaced people to come back to their neighborhoods and give also breathing room for the civic societies so they can operate in the areas that are not able to do that right now.

Mr. KINZINGER. Understood.

And, Ms. Romero, do you have any comments on that?

Ms. ROMERO. Yeah. I mean, I have to be boring and say we have to be impartial, too.

Mr. KINZINGER. I understand.

Ms. ROMERO. However, I will add a couple of things.

Mr. KINZINGER. It is not boring. It is okay.

Ms. ROMERO. We have been calling for humanitarian ceasefires and pauses, because we share the view, yeah, we need to be able to get through, and insecurity means that we are not able to get through with aid. So we do need measures taken by both parties to the conflict, or more than both—than two at this point to allow access to civilian populations to deliver aid.

But no-fly zones, humanitarian corridors, all of those, they have had mixed results in the past. We would urge that if they are looked at, that we consider past experiences, that we learn from those lessons and weigh whatever the benefits are against the cost to civilians.

Mr. KINZINGER. Thank you.

And, Madam Chair, there are 180,000 people that have died in this conflict and, sadly, more to come that I would believe if they could today would thank you for having this hearing. I yield back.

Ms. ROS-LEHTINEN. Thank you very much, sir. Thank you.

The chair recognizes herself for some other questions, if that is okay. Mr. Deutch will later as well.

How much of your work is done primarily through middlemen or through direct assistance? And if you use intermediaries, what sort of vetting process do you have that—not that you can guarantee that the aid will get to the right people, but how do you manage that? Ms. Koppel.

Ms. KOPPEL. Madam Chairwoman, thank you for the question. We have a "do no harm" approach under guiding humanitarian principles, as we have said, of independence and impartiality. Mercy Corps has been working inside Syria for the last almost 2 years, and while we did have some expatriate staff working inside the country, as it became more dangerous, they have had to withdraw. And our staff are entirely Mercy Corps staff, but they are almost 100 percent Syrian, and so we work directly with them.

Our reviews and the compliance and accountability that we put in place with all of our employees is of the highest standards. We ask, when we are working through these relief committees and through community-based organizations, that they provide us with a list of the most vulnerable people. We then vet that list with them. We have Mercy Corps staff that are there for at least 60 percent of the distributions that take place. We then follow up after the distribution with a random sampling of about 5 percent of the people who receive the aid to ensure that in fact they were the ones who got it.

We have other standards in place such that if any check is going to be signed, the person who made the—who issued the—for example, if it was a purchase of some kind, that they are not the one, then, who follows up to ensure that the money was paid to the right vendor. There are three people who would be involved in that, all of whom were not engaged in the initial procurement.

Following up after a distribution, we usually then have every 3 to 4 months meetings with the civil society actors, the relief committees to see how things are going, to get feedback from them, and to ensure that we are able to adapt as we go.

We also make sure from the outset that our partners know that we will not allow, if we have any sense and an inkling that there is divergence of aid or the possibility of divergence of aid, Mercy Corps will not work in that neighborhood. So—and the other piece is that we do not negotiate with any armed actors. So we are only working with civilians and people from the community.

Ms. ROS-LEHTINEN. Very clear. Thank you.

Anyone else? Ms. Solberg and then Dr. Sahloul.

Ms. SOLBERG. Sure. Thank you, Madam Chairwoman. I would just say in terms of our work in Syria, we are working through partners, through local partners who we identify through a process of referrals. We carry out very, very in-depth due diligence processes, and, again, following our humanitarian principles, and we do a lot of capacity building and working hand in hand with those partners.

We also have developed third-party monitoring systems, which, in fact, we are sharing with other humanitarian organizations who are doing work in Syria as well, so we can learn from each other and really also trying to strengthen the coordination amongst the different organizations who are working in Syria.

In terms of our refugee programming, we do direct implementation ourselves as well as working with partners to do—and a lot of that has to do with making sure we are identifying the differing needs of women, men, boys and girls. And we also enlist the—or give opportunities for Syrian refugees to also volunteer and be participants in our programming in our urban refugee centers.

Ms. ROS-LEHTINEN. Congratulations.

Ms. Wanek.

Ms. WANEK. Thank you. I just wanted to add in as well the dynamic of speaking about Lebanon as well when we speak of this crisis. Global Communities also strictly adheres to all the U.S. legal and regulatory requirements to ensure that no support is given to any organization or person that is in any way connected to terrorism.

So some of the ways that we ensure this compliance would be through the vetting of all organizations and individuals with which we work through the U.S. Treasury's Office of Foreign Assets Control, or OFAC, through the System for Award Management, or SAM, and any U.N. sanction lists, as well as being vigilant and following all executive orders and other legal parameters that prohibit transactions with a provision to aid to those associated with terrorism.

And I think it is important as well to note that we have been working in Lebanon, for example, since 1997, and so being very much present in the communities, having a community-based approach very much makes it possible for us to rely on the deep knowledge of the people that we work with to ensure that the assistance that we are providing there goes exactly where we want it to.

Ms. ROS-LEHTINEN. Very good. Thank you.

Doctor?

Dr. SAHLOUL. I just want to mention that the Syrian American Medical Society, or SAMS, besides sending medical missions, we have about 120 of our physicians who went into medical missions in the last year or so, but we also send medical supplies. In the United States, we have about 1,600 members who are members of the Syrian American healthcare professionals, but we have regional offices in Turkey, Lebanon and Jordan. For example, the Cuban American community sent about 4 tons of medical supplies with our help. So we sent it—we have an agreement with the Turkish Red Crescent, that they will receive these supplies, they will put it on the border, and then our network inside Syria will take the supplies and distribute it to hospitals in Aleppo. We take pictures, we take reports, we take—and our network also tracks the numbers of patients who are benefited. And we have extensive reporting, because we are responsible to our funders, to our donors and also to the grantees. Some of them are United States aid, of course, organizations. And we have several ways to make sure that every piece of equipment or supply that is sent is also reported and documented to our donors and to our funders.

Ms. ROS-LEHTINEN. Thank you so much, Doctor.

Ms. Romero.

Ms. ROMERO. Yes. Similar to our colleague organizations, we have a mix of direct implementation. We also work with ministries of health and education and their local offices, and we work through partners. Where we have a history of working, we are working with organizations that we have worked with for a long time and ministries that we have worked with for a long time, but we do have vetting and other standards for vendors and for other partners that we work with, as well as evaluation and monitoring mechanisms.

Ms. ROS-LEHTINEN. Thank you to all of you.

Mr. Deutch.

Mr. DEUTCH. Thanks, Madam Chairman.

I wanted to get back to the broader funding issue. I am appalled by the lack of response to the U.N. appeal. And a number of you have spoken generally about the need to speak up and push to ensure that others from around the globe are meeting their obligations. Can you speak in—can you be more direct? Where can we be the most helpful? Who should be doing more? Who isn't? What is the rationale? How do we engage in this in a way that will actually ensure that others do what needs to be done in order to help address this dire situation?

Any of you. Yes, Ms. Wanek.

Ms. WANEK. I think an important tenet that we need to face this with is to sort of understand that prevention is cheaper than intervention, that very much we need to approach this as these are just the types of issues that we can approach now to provide the humanitarian assistance that is needed to be able to somewhat stabilize what could really be a critical situation out there between refugees and host communities. So, I mean, I would continue to ask for you to put pressure on your colleagues and on other governments to uphold their pledges.

Mr. DEUTCH. Okay.

Dr. Sahloul.

Dr. SAHLOUL. A couple of comments. First of all, I just want to make sure that we make sure that our administration appreciates the effort that is done by the neighboring countries, especially the

Government of Turkey, because they have spent $3 billion for refugees. The healthcare provided is for free education. It is for free. It is a model country in terms of hosting refugees. Of course, to some extent also the same thing with the Government of Jordan and Lebanon and Iraq. Lebanon probably is the most needy country among the four neighboring countries in terms of Syria, because the scale of the refugees and the fact that it has limited resources, followed by Jordan.

I think we need leadership from our administration, because the funders or the countries that are able to fund the humanitarian assistance listen to what we have to say. So if we pressure the Gulf countries, for example, and tell them, why don't you increase your support, and they have done it before when we asked them to do that, I think they will increase their support; maybe not through the United Nations, because they are hesitant to send supplies or assistance that will go through the regime ways, but maybe through other NGO's.

Mr. DEUTCH. So just play that out a little bit, the difference between funding through—funding through the NGO's and governments and the U.N. What is—how best to engage the countries? Look, it is the request was for $6.5 billion for this year, right, and just over $1 billion has been pledged. Now, the balance of that— you are not telling me the balance of that—they haven't stepped to the—they haven't stepped to the table with the balance of that, because they don't like where the money is going?

Dr. SAHLOUL. Well, that is part of the issue, in my view, that they feel that the assistance that is provided through the United Nation agencies are going only through the regime-controlled areas. I mean, I can tell you that you have people died of starvation 10 minutes away from the United Nations headquarters in Damascus, and when people hear these reports and see the pictures of patients dying of starvation 10 minutes away from the heart of Damascus and you have all of United Nations agencies in the heart of Damascus, they will be hesitant to support these operations. But they know, for example, that other NGO's that are going through the borders from Jordan or Turkey are able to reach any population, of course, except for the population who are under complete siege; that is very difficult to get to them. There are 250,000 people who are under siege at this point.

Mr. DEUTCH. Ms. Romero, you had, I think, spoken, not as directly as I hope you might now, about where we might exert that pressure to be useful.

Ms. ROMERO. Yeah. I mean, I agree more pressure on the Gulf probably makes sense, but I was just looking at the list in front of me of who has funded and who hasn't. And, you know, traditionally we have really kind of relied on Europe to kind of step up and be the next big humanitarian donor. With the crisis there, I think, unfortunately, we are in a place where we are being expected to give a bit more, but some countries have been less affected by the crisis there, you know, are quite low, Norway, Finland, or going to further south out of Europe, Australia hasn't given that much.

So I think, you know, we can look at some traditional allies that have given generously to other crises and to other parts of the world and really target our diplomatic pressure in that way.

Mr. DEUTCH. And in the past, who has taken—who has taken the lead in galvanizing the support for addressing other crises?

Ms. ROMERO. I would say the U.S., the U.K. and ECHO, the European Commission.

Mr. DEUTCH. Anyone else? All right.

I would appreciate it, if there are some specific suggestions that you would be more comfortable making in a different setting, I hope that you will feel free to reach out to us, because there is such an enormous amount that needs to be done, all of you, again, know better than anyone.

And, Madam Chairman, it is disheartening for us to have these hearings as often as we have to, but the fact is that the situation on the ground is only going to worsen, so I commend you for calling this hearing and I appreciate the time.

Ms. ROS-LEHTINEN. Thank you, Mr. Deutch. And what was that phrase that you used, the numbness, psychic——

Mr. DEUTCH. Psychic numbing.

Ms. ROS-LEHTINEN. Numbing.

Mr. DEUTCH. Is what——

Ms. ROS-LEHTINEN. Yes. I think that what we see—because it is sort of like a Whac-A-Mole foreign policy crises. We are sending 80 boots on the ground to Nigeria, as well we should—it is a terrible situation—but we move from crisis to crisis, and we have forgotten what stirred our conscience just as recently as this terrible situation, humanitarian crisis in Syria, and now we are focused elsewhere, and it seems that we do have some of that psychic numbing, but we can do better. We must do better.

Thank you. Thank you for being here. Thank you for your testimony. Thank you to your organizations. Those caregivers, those workers, what they do day in and day out, it is inspiring. So thank you very much. And with that, this hearing is adjourned.

[Whereupon, at 3:48 p.m., the subcommittee was adjourned.]

APPENDIX

MATERIAL SUBMITTED FOR THE RECORD

SUBCOMMITTEE HEARING NOTICE
COMMITTEE ON FOREIGN AFFAIRS
U.S. HOUSE OF REPRESENTATIVES
WASHINGTON, DC 20515-6128

Subcommittee on the Middle East and North Africa
Ileana Ros-Lehtinen (R-FL), Chairman

May 16, 2014

TO: MEMBERS OF THE COMMITTEE ON FOREIGN AFFAIRS

You are respectfully requested to attend an OPEN hearing of the Committee on Foreign Affairs, to be held by the Subcommittee on the Middle East and North Africa in Room 2172 of the Rayburn House Office Building (and available live on the Committee website at www.foreignaffairs.house.gov):

DATE: Wednesday, May 21, 2014

TIME: 2:00 p.m.

SUBJECT: The Humanitarian Crisis in Syria: Views from the Ground

WITNESSES: Ms. Andrea Koppel
Vice President of Global Engagement and Policy
Mercy Corps

Ms. Holly Solberg
Director of Emergency and Humanitarian Assistance
CARE

Ms. Pia Wanek
Director
Office of Humanitarian Assistance
Global Communities

Mr. Zaher Sahloul, M.D.
President
Syrian American Medical Society

Ms. Bernice Romero
Senior Director of Policy and Advocacy
Save the Children

By Direction of the Chairman

COMMITTEE ON FOREIGN AFFAIRS

MINUTES OF SUBCOMMITTEE ON _____ *Middle East and North Africa* _____ HEARING

Day___*Wednesday*___Date_____*05/21/14*_____Room_____*2172*_____

Starting Time ____*2:00 p.m.*___ Ending Time ___*3:48 p.m.*_____

Recesses ___*1*___ (*2:15* to *2:45*) (____to____) (____to____) (____to____) (____to____) (____to____)

Presiding Member(s)

Chairman Ros-Lehtinen

Check all of the following that apply:

Open Session ☑
Executive (closed) Session ☐
Televised ☑

Electronically Recorded (taped) ☑
Stenographic Record ☑

TITLE OF HEARING:

The Humanitarian Crisis in Syria: Views from the Ground

SUBCOMMITTEE MEMBERS PRESENT:

Chairman Ros-Lehtinen, Ranking Member Deutch, Reps. Chabot, Kinzinger, Cotton, and Schneider

---

NON-SUBCOMMITTEE MEMBERS PRESENT: *(Mark with an * if they are not members of full committee.)*

Chairman Royce

HEARING WITNESSES: Same as meeting notice attached? Yes ☑ No ☐
(If "no", please list below and include title, agency, department, or organization.)

STATEMENTS FOR THE RECORD: *(List any statements submitted for the record.)*

SFR - Rep. Connolly

TIME SCHEDULED TO RECONVENE _____
or
TIME ADJOURNED ___*3:48 p.m.*_____

Subcommittee Staff Director

Statement for the Record
Submitted by the Honorable Gerald E. Connolly

The crisis in Syria is now in its fourth year, and the mass atrocities perpetrated by the regime of President Bashar al-Assad on the civilian population -- including sectarian violence, mass killings, torture, and bombings -- show no signs of subsiding. The U.S. and its international partners have grown increasingly impatient with efforts by the Assad regime to deny access for United Nations humanitarian assistance, and earlier this month, the Emergency Relief Coordinator for the UN confirmed our worst fears, saying, "far from getting better, the situation is getting worse."

Indeed, the number of refugees has grown four times larger than it was last year, which USAID Administrator Shah has called, "unprecedented." More than 40% of Syria's population is in need of humanitarian assistance with 6 million displaced internally and another 3 million refugees dispersed across Lebanon, Turkey, Jordan, and other countries in the region. Basic food and medical supplies have been blocked, relief workers and vehicles have been attacked, and some UN staff members are still being detained by Syrian forces. A recent UN report assessing compliance with a Security Council resolution ordering the free flow of assistance to civilians cites the Assad regime and its supporters for clear violations of international humanitarian law.

As if that weren't troubling enough, we're now seeing reports alleging the Assad regime has used chlorine gas bombs in more than a dozen attacks on civilians in recent months. I understand Secretary Kerry has reviewed the raw evidence in these cases and that the Organization for the Prohibition of Chemical Weapons (OPCW) has launched an investigation. The OPCW also is overseeing the disposal of Syria's chemical weapons stockpile under the agreement brokered last fall, and it reports that Syria has shipped or destroyed 92% of the weapons it pledged to eliminate. However, chlorine gas was not on the list of chemicals the Assad regime supplied to regulators. If these latest reports are true, Assad will have breached the Chemical Weapons Convention, which it signed as part of last year's agreement.

These troubling developments, coupled with the recent resignation of the UN's chief mediator for Syria, veteran Algerian diplomat Lakhdar Brahimi, underscore the importance of this Committee's action two weeks ago in reporting a pair of resolutions aimed at giving greater urgency to U.S. engagement in Syria. H. Res. 520 directs the President to report back to Congress within 60 days on a new strategy to address the mounting humanitarian disaster, and H. Con. Res. 51 lends support for investigating and prosecuting war crimes in Syria. France already has called on the UN to refer Syria the International Criminal Court based on the recent chlorine bomb allegations.

I look forward to hearing from today's panel about what more can and should be done to improve conditions on the ground for the millions of displaced civilians inside Syria while we await additional steps to be taken. It is clear current humanitarian efforts have fallen short, overwhelmed by the magnitude of the challenge.